Portfolio Management for Private Wealth

An Introduction to Portfolio Theory and Practice

Jesse Picunko, CFA

Portfolio Management for Private Wealth

ISBN 979-8-524-75095-2

To my wife Jaime,
who has had far more faith in me than I did,
and who contributed the cover art to this book

Contents

INTRODUCTION 1

PART ONE: WHAT ARE YOU DOING? 4

    WEALTH MANAGEMENT VS PORTFOLIO MANAGEMENT 4

    THE FINANCIAL PLAN 8

    MONTE CARLO SIMULATION AND PLANNING 13

    ALLOCATION 17

PART TWO: PORTFOLIO THEORY 19

    PORTFOLIO DEFINITION 19

    PORTFOLIO CONSTRUCTION – GOAL AND CONSTRANTS 21

    RISK 23

    VOLATILITY 25

    JARGON 30

    EFFICIENT MARKETS AND RANDOM WALKS 32

    MODERN PORTFOLIO THEORY 35

    THE EFFICIENT FRONTIER 39

    CAPITAL MARKET LINE 42

    THE MARKET PORTFOLIO 45

    SYSTEMATIC RISK, UNSYSTEMATIC RISK, AND BETA 47

    BETA 48

PART THREE: THE CONSTRUCTION PROCESS 51

    BENCHMARK DEFINITION 51

    ALPHA AND RISK-ADJUSTED RETURN 54

    SHARPE RATIO 56

    THE OPTION SET OF COMPENSATED RISK 58

    EQUITIES 60

    EQUITY INVESTING 64

    FIXED INCOME – BASICS 68

    FIXED INCOME – USES 72

    FIXED INCOME INVESTING 75

    INFLATION 81

    ALTERNATIVE INVESTMENTS 87

    ALTERNATIVE INVESTMENTS – PRIVATE EQUITY 89

    ALTERNATIVE INVESTMENTS – HEDGE FUNDS 92

ALTERNATIVE INVESTMENTS – RISK PARITY 98

PUTTING IT TOGETHER 102

PART FOUR: THE BUILDING BLOCKS 104

HOW YOU GET THERE – ALLOCATION AND ASSESSMENT 104

LEVERS 106

FACTORS 108

USING FACTORS 113

PULLING LEVERS 115

ALPHA VS BETA – IT'S ALL IN THE BENCHMARK 121

BUILDING THE PORTFOLIO 123

PART FIVE: MONITORING AND REPORTING 127

RETURN ATTRIBUTION AND MONITORING 127

TRACKING ERROR 135

EVALUATING MANAGERS – What are they doing? 139

EVALUATING MANAGERS – How are they doing it? 143

CONSEQUENCES OF AN INFORMATION DEFICIT 146

PART SIX: MANAGING MONEY 149

DEVELOPING A WORLD VIEW 149

MARKETS AND VALUATION 151

MANAGING YOUR ANGLE OF ATTACK – BIAS VS PROCESS 154

TACTICAL / STRATEGIC 156

OFFENSE / DEFENSE AND RISK BUDGET 158

PLAN FOR OPPORTUNITIES 160

BOTTOM UP / TOP DOWN 162

HEDGING VS MARKET TIMING 164

LONG HORIZON AND SHORT TERM RESULTS 166

FINDING AN AESTHETIC 168

MENTAL MISTAKES AND BEHAVIORAL FINANCE 170

MULTI-ASSET PORTFOLIO MANAGEMENT 172

WHAT COLOR IS YOUR PORTFOLIO? 174

THE MANAGEMENT EXPERIENCE 177

INTRODUCTION

The practice of Portfolio Management is not Wealth Management, despite how close the two terms sound. Portfolio Management is a discipline that could be extremely granular, with attention paid to minute details of risk, security selection, and correlation. Or it could be a broadly thematic exercise, hovering close to passive themes and allowing the markets to do the heavy lifting. But even at its most relaxed, investing should never be accidental. It should be informed, methodical, and purposeful. I have heard a financial advisor tell a client, "investing is the easy part." Indeed, it is easy to push buttons and move money. But that should not be considered professional investment management.

I used to manage bond portfolios for a large pension fund. As an institutional fixed income manager, an academic approach to management comes automatically as you track performance by the basis point. I believe most bond investors have a well thumbed-through Fabozzi textbook easily within reach. Additionally, when you have 200+ line items with nondescript names, you are less attached to any one bond. What matters is how all these bonds work together to shape your portfolio. You are not in love with a name, but the process. When I transitioned to a private wealth role and was surprised by many things. I was initially embarrassed by my own insular perspective, but then confused by the lack of process I was familiar with on the institutional side.

Multi-asset portfolios built for individual clients should have a similar rigor of process. For a client with a 20- or 30- year time horizon, *whether* you owned stocks matters much more than which stocks you owned. The long horizon allows many things to happen: short term volatility becomes a long term return history, your winners and losers may balance out towards a market return, and your decisions that are made from a process are more likely to keep you moving forward.

One night as a freshman in college, I had missed the midnight deadline for a computer science program and I was visibly frustrated. A friend of mine in the class asked me a question. "Can you control it?" I thought for a second. "I guess I could study more for the final and get my grade up."

1

"Then don't worry about it!" he said. "And if you can't control it, don't worry about it!"

We have illusions that we can tame this market monster but quickly learn it's not so simple. This book is about portfolio construction and management. It is about taking control of what you *can* control, and letting go of the rest. It is about making conscious decisions about how to invest, how much risk to take, and how to be guided towards what is in your power to effect. As a portfolio manager, making trades then nail biting while waiting for them to be right (or through the times they are wrong) can be harrowing. Some people choose to make their trades and close their eyes, hoping to be proven right at some point down the road. Or they avert their eyes, expecting the trade to be correct at commencement and requiring no oversight. Others barely make any trades, afraid of the timing or the appearance of being active and wrong. This book will help you think of the management process holistically with each adjustment an expression of a viewpoint, or a reduction of risk. It will make each trade easier because it fits a broader narrative – a portfolio that speaks as a sum of its parts.

Unfortunately we make mistakes as investors. But learning through errors creates very strong reflexes for the future. This book discusses how goal-setting and rear-view analysis can help you avoid future potholes in performance, and how to learn to absorb information that leads to actionable ideas. Good traders and portfolio managers make mistakes just like everyone else; they just make fewer stupid ones.

Through taking control and using market feedback, we become better at investing. This book will hopefully show you how to think about these concepts to refine your portfolio management style. It will help you think about what success looks like for you and your clients. And it will give you the language to articulate your process. With these tools you can take some seeming randomness away from the market and define your own path.

There are a lot of things this book is not. It is not a book about investing and generating alpha. That sounds odd, but I argue that portfolio management is a different discipline than security selection. For multi-asset portfolio managers, which is essentially what a financial advisor is, the capacity for expertise in each product is limited. This book is targeted for those who are compiling the expertise of outside managers but need a better understanding of how to put it all together.

There are parts of this text that will be challenging for some, and elementary for others. I hope there is enough in here that would be worthy of those who know most of these concepts, and accessible for those who know none of it.

The impetus of this book was my observation of a single advisor investing all of his clients in a mutual fund with a beta of 60%, and despite a decade of underperformance his insistence that it had superior risk-adjusted returns.[1] I realized that explaining why it was inappropriate required a fairly complex explanation. The discussion that begins with a client's goals, continues to the usefulness of market sensitivity, and then to portfolio construction and evaluation is actually very long – and I don't think I've seen it presented from a practical standpoint. Though I don't want to bludgeon the reader with theory, there is a linear path from how we talk about portfolios academically to how we actually manage them.

I wish this book didn't need to exist, but I've seen far too many prospects' portfolios butchered by an advisor's lack of knowledge, lack of planning, or lack of integrity. Though no book can protect a client from malfeasance, I do hope that young advisors, struggling to figure it all out, can use these concepts to put their clients in a better place.

---

[1] All of these terms will be discussed throughout the book.

PART ONE: WHAT ARE YOU DOING?
WEALTH MANAGEMENT VS PORTFOLIO MANAGEMENT

It is important to realize there is a difference between wealth management and portfolio management. While most practitioners would use the term interchangeably, they are simply different disciplines.

The Wealth Manager

A competent wealth manager must think holistically about his client. He must be aware of a client's long term goals, estate plans, tax situation, and every detail that relates to their financial preparedness. The wealth manager should ensure competent management of each aspect, quarterback the operations, and anticipate needs. Should these accounts be set up as trusts? Can we harvest tax losses? Are the kids' college funding plans in place?

Necessarily, a successful wealth manager, who is able to garner clients' trust, is a communicator. Their ability to demonstrate empathy and understanding draws clients to reveal their concerns and needs. They are meticulous, able to manage multiple financial relationships so the client never needs to check status. They are confident, able to guide clients and calm their nerves through difficult times. It should also be noted that successful financial advisors are probably capable salesmen, who can think on their feet, adapt to a conversation, and enjoy the networking required to build a business.

The wealth manager uses his ability to communicate to extract information so every detail can be addressed. Creating deep relationships helps the advisor anticipate situations, protect clients from pitfalls, and be a sounding board for advice. With this information, a financial plan can be formed that is as thorough as it needs to be.

Wealth managers must have some expertise in many different disciplines. They must have a firm grasp of accounting and taxes. They must know more than the tax implications of trading but be able to offer some knowledge and advice. From simple concepts like IRA to Roth conversions and more complicated structures like the benefits of charitable remainder trusts. Wealth managers should understand how to interact with estate attorneys and know which clients could benefit from more complex estate planning. They must have a good grasp of insurance products and know how gaps in coverage could be bridged, and when they offer an advantage over traditional investments. The breadth of knowledge an investment manager must be exposed to (or have access to) should be intimidating to a newcomer to the business. Every client conversation could draw on any of these disciplines, and the ability to realize a client's needs and generate solutions is a core value provided by the wealth manager.

The job of wealth manager is *difficult.* Not because every client is a problem, but because every problem is your job to solve. Sometimes tedious, often intractable. For instance, a client could have assets tied up in real estate but has short term funding needs that must be met. Or as another example, a client has life insurance products that need to be replaced but communication breaks down between the carriers and the client. There are endless ways advisors find themselves in the middle, and their only role is to ensure both sides are working towards resolution.

With perhaps hundreds of client relationships it is hard to keep every client's need front and center. Foresight is a crucial characteristic of a wealth manager. Being able to know what comes next to game out a possible landmined future and find a smooth path is a crucial skill.

Clients engage a wealth manager to navigate their financial complexities. It is when things are difficult the wealth manager earns their fees, and the client expects a seamless integration and flow of their affairs. They are expected to be available for thoughtful advice on all manner of decisions; from household insurance suggestions to mortgage refinancing and loan options. The breadth of knowledge and detail obsession required is hard to provide. By comparison, investment management misleadingly seems myopic compared to everything else because the process looks straightforward – deploy cash into securities and wait for them to perform. Of course it *should* be more difficult than that, and clients expect more expertise managing investments as managing their finances.

The Portfolio Manager

If a portfolio manager had a proverbial crystal ball it would be an easier job. The reality is, however, that portfolio management is rather a slower, more methodical, and ongoing undertaking of trying to understand the present with guidance from the past.

To the extent that a financial advisor is exercising discretionary control of a client's investment positions, the advisor must understand a client's expectation of them. It may not be articulated because clients assume it's true: that the advisor actually knows how to manage portfolios. Unfortunately this is not always the case. Prior to the turn of the 21st century there was little ambiguity about who was on the other side of the call: a stockbroker selling a brokerage house's trading and research capabilities. One would never expect that person to manage an individual's portfolio. But research was corrupted and devalued by conflicts of interest, revealed convincingly by the dot.com crisis when favorable sell-side research was used to win banking business. Furthermore, discount brokers took volume from the full service operations. Commissions for trading were eventually replaced by the "wrap fee," where clients paid a single assets under management fee for "advice" and those stock brokers now had new titles to reflect the new orientation of the service provided.

In many cases, missing from that transition was a credible education system that taught the basics of portfolio management. Unfortunately I have seen too many client portfolios that have been bludgeoned by the inexperience, indifference, and avarice of their advisors – where training is focused on networking tactics, sales quotas, and high up-front commission products instead of education. Though many investment managers are endowed with vast internal resources, a firehose of research is not a substitute for a discussion on building intelligent portfolios.

Many Registered Investment Advisors (RIAs) state they are fully educated about investment process and adhere to the **Fiduciary Standard** which places client interests above their own (this compares to the "**Suitability**" requirement that brokers are subject to – any product that is suitable can be offered regardless of whether it is the best.) Unfortunately, many advisors do not have the depth of experience, skills, and knowledge that they present.

This work is not meant to paint a broad brush and indict the industry. Rather I want to bridge a gap in the literature. Much of what is written for wealth portfolio management ignores the practical implications of theory and the construction tools and methods common in the institutional setting. Institutional investors employ sophisticated portfolio management tools, and are often educated with specialized investment-centric training programs like the Chartered Financial Analyst (CFA) designation and trained in the use of their analytical tools. In short, they have the backing and support to dig into their investment decisions and processes. Meanwhile, those starting at the bottom in the individual client business are given a phone and a call list. This book is written with them in mind, though I hope successful veterans can still glean some insight from these pages.

The skills that would propel a financial advisor to success are quite different from a portfolio manager. The Portfolio Managers should have an affection and respect for the financial markets. They should have a comfort level with statistics and data and an ability to build an analysis from scratch. Though there are many portfolio management systems in the market place with extraordinary capabilities, being able to imagine a problem and illustrate it in Microsoft Excel can be just as crucial. Portfolio managers should have a curiosity and hunger for information. An investment decision is always made with less information than you would like. That does not mean you close your eyes and pounce, it means you keep searching until you are satisfied you have gone as far as you can.

Portfolio management is a *persistent* process that begins with identifying problems that investment assets can solve, follows with a thoughtful design, and continues *forever* with a monitoring, evaluating, and rebalancing regime. Portfolio management does not end when you have entered trade tickets.

Anyone who tackles the role of financial advisor and investment manager should be aware of the mental commitment and time requirements to perform both responsibly. Because it is mechanically simple to place assets some assume it is easy to invest. They pick funds from an approved list, dazzled by good marketing. Some financial advisors abdicate their responsibility for portfolio management. One advisor wrote in a newsletter that **alpha** (performance) was not his responsibility – it was the job of the funds or managers with which he invested.

It should be clear – taking the mandate from a client to manage their money is a promise to deliver constant oversight and to take responsibility for the results.

Retirement planning can begin with a rule of thumb known as the 4% rule. This rule, developed by financial advisor William Bengen, suggests that retirees can safely withdraw 4% of their portfolio and maintain their lifestyle over their retirement years, even accounting for inflation. Given a 4% rate of withdrawal, one can deduce that an appropriate portfolio size at retirement would be 25 times your needed annual funds for expenses (in excess of retirement income sources like social security.) Bengen developed his rule by looking at the historical experience of a 50% stocks, 50% bonds portfolio over every 30 year period since 1926[2]. Bengen discovered that 4% was the highest withdrawal rate that ensured the retiree would have enough retirement resources for any rolling 30 year period. But there are many variables that make this rule of thumb subject to adjustment. How much of the portfolio is taxable upon withdrawal? What if the client preferred a higher allocation to stocks? What if the client intended to retire early, or expected a longer lifespan? There are many circumstances that would make the 4% rule inadequate, and for that reason we build detailed financial plans for clients.[3]

Though the practice of wealth management and portfolio management can diverge, the two disciplines come together at the Financial Plan. The financial plan is the roadmap from today to the "end of plan" – a euphemism for the death of clients. The plan seeks to identify all sources of income and savings and tries to anticipate likely spending activity. Ultimately, the goal is to track a feasible amount of retirement lifestyle spending, suggest a reasonable retirement age, or project a legacy that would be available upon death. Any of those goals necessarily impact the feasibility of the others, so clients are confronted with what they are willing to accept for their lifetime goals. It is like pressing on a balloon, causing it to push out in other places. There are finite resources but a myriad of wants.

---

[2] In other words, Bergen observed the performance of a portfolio from 1926 – 1955, then 1927 – 1956, then 1928 – 1957, etc and found a 4% withdrawal rate (adjusting for inflation) was the maximum that could be withdrawn without depleting the portfolio in every 30-year scenario.

[3] Many advisors misunderstand the 4% rule, describing it as an annuity rate a client can withdraw from indefinitely. Also, if an advisor charged a 1% fee, the client could only draw 3% for their own needs.

Not long ago I thought the concept strange – given how many unknowns there are between now and my retirement age – decades to go. The value of the exercise seemed academic but not useful. And yet, there are enough assumptions to flesh out the future. How much are you saving? Do you expect to pay children's college expenses? What is your household budget like? How big is your current portfolio? Although not an exhaustive list of questions, with just that much information I can **estimate** how much I could conceivably give towards my childrens' education and still have a comfortable retirement. Or if I decide to move into a larger house, I can observe how much a change in my current budget impacts my future ability to spend. I emphasize this is a constantly changing estimate, but armed with information I can make changes and adjust as unforeseen events occur. Without that guidance, how would I know what would need to be changed? **Crucially, the financial plan can also show how much you are relying on return from the portfolio for future expenses.**

I like to think of the financial plan as a tool that squares what is feasible to spend in retirement with what is possible to earn and save beforehand. No, we do not know how much money we will have, nor how much we will spend decades from now. However we can make reasonable projections given our current income and how much we *could* potentially spend, as it impacts our decisions today. If we know that our investment income and return will provide the bulk of our resources, we may find that a higher allocation to stocks is required to meet our needs. If we find that we have ample income to satisfy lifestyle demands, a higher allocation to bonds may be prudent.

The financial plan details a path along which we can guide our clients towards their retirement years. This path serves many purposes. It helps make sure investments are directed towards the appropriate goal. It is a reminder to control spending and save what is needed. It shows you what large expenditures can be accommodated. Without having the path in view those questions are more difficult to answer.

Illustration of a simple financial plan

A plan analysis **begins** with a review of the assumptions the plan makes, which should include the following (though not an exhaustive list):
- A retirement age that reflects the client's expectation

- A spending plan in retirement that is reasonable given the client's lifestyle
- An estimate of the savings the client can generate each year before retirement[4]
- Key spending needs that may occur along the way (college education, new cars, travel)
- An assumed inflation rate

Next we should itemize the resources available as this helps clarify what is possible. Investment accounts, real estate income, social security expectations, pensions, and other sources of retirement income are included.

Let's consider a sample client:
Current age: 64
Current portfolio: $1,000,000 invested 60% stocks and 40% bonds
Current savings per annum: $80,000 / year[5]
Retirement lifestyle spending: $100,000 annually with a 2% inflation rate

For simplicity we ignore taxes and Social Security income but in reality these are crucial components of the plan. For illustrative purposes we will assume that stocks have an expected return of 8% and bonds have an expected return of 2%. For this portfolio, the expected return is hence 5.6%.[6]

---

[4] For simplicity this savings number encompasses the entire budget – after tax income less typical uses of income
[5] Savings are assumed to be invested and generating growth for the plan. An investor should be cognizant of "Asset Location" and maximize tax deferred contributions where possible
[6] 8% return on equities X 60% allocation to equities + 2% return on bonds X 40% allocation to bonds

With this information we can play out next year's financial profile:

	Starting Portfolio	Savings	Investment Return	Retirement Spending	Ending Portfolio
Age 64	$1,000,000	$80,0000	$56,000	$0	$1,136,000

Now let's assume the client retires at Age 65

	Starting Portfolio	Savings	Investment Return	Retirement Spending	Ending Portfolio
Age 65	$1,136,000	$0	$63,616	$100,000	$1,099,616
Age 66	$1,099,616	$0	$61,578	$102,000	$1,061,194
Age 67	$1,061,194	$0	$59,427	$104,040	$1,016,581

Notice the portfolio is shrinking rapidly.

By Age 79 the profile looks like this:

	Starting Portfolio	Savings	Investment Return	Retirement Spending	Ending Portfolio
Age 79	$148,524	$0	$8,317	$131,948	$24,894

The bottom line is this client will be out of money by age 80. Given longer lifespans that people are living the prospect of being destitute by then is not an acceptable option.

We clearly don't know everything that will happen to this client between now and age 80, but we do know this financial plan will fail with these assumptions and we need to encourage the client to make adjustments such as the following four actions:

- reduce his expected spending
- increase his retirement age
- increase how much he saves before retirement
- increase his allocation to stocks to generate higher portfolio expected returns.

Where there is room to maneuver we can hold something constant and solve for the needed adjustment. For example, holding retirement spending unchanged, how much more would we need to save before retirement? Or the opposite – solve for how much future spending can the current savings rate currently support. How much does delaying retirement improve the plan? Finally, how much more spending can we afford if we earned more on the portfolio?

The first three actions above are uncontroversial. The fourth, however, is an explicit embrace of risk to improve the expected future outlook. This is where portfolio management and wealth management have a moment of intersection. With this information, the financial advisor knows how much risk the client needs to take. Too much risk creates vulnerabilities in case of a market downturn. ***Too little risk can make the financial plan unviable.*** In this way, once the client agrees with the fundamentals of the plan **including the portfolio risk profile**, the financial plan becomes the portfolio manager's North Star. It is the **neutral** position.

When we are using only the expected return on investment we get the most likely path. Another approach to calibrating the financial plan uses statistics to calculate the "probability of success." Because the investment return is not guaranteed, we are dealing with probabilities and estimates. Most financial planning software will run multiple statistical paths for each year's investment return in the plan. Sometimes returns may be high, sometimes they may be negative. Adding return volatility of the assets in the portfolio we can calculate the probability of achieving less desirable outcomes. This technique is known as Monte Carlo simulation.

Students of statistics would be familiar with the normal distribution, the bell-shaped curve that shows the likelihood of an event around the average in a sample of data. It plots how often data occurs on the y-axis and the range of the data along the x-axis. The middle, highest part of the curve is the most likely scenario and where the curve tapers on either side is called the tails. For our purposes here, the sample is the distribution of possible retirement outcomes, either the value of the portfolio at "end of plan" or the retirement lifestyle spending the portfolio could support without being depleted. What we are concerned with is the left tail - the probability that the highest feasible post-retirement lifestyle expenditure is below what a client would like to live on.

If we could rely on long-term returns then we would not be as concerned with a few bad years. A static portfolio with no withdrawals would grow at the average growth rate regardless of the order of good years and bad years. The Standard & Poor's 500 (S&P 500) index is a widely-quoted gauge of US Large-Capitalization stock performance. The index has historically returned over 8% per annum on average and very few rolling ten-year periods would be difficult for an investor to weather given that assumption. For a portfolio with no contributions or distributions, the total return is unaffected by the order of each year's returns. -40%, +80%, -20%, +60% would have the same result as +60%, +80%, -40%, and -20%. Money lost in market weakness is returned during periods of market strength. However, if those first few years looked like -40% and -20%, during which you were withdrawing at market lows the losses on funds withdrawn can never be recovered.

For this reason Monte Carlo simulation can be used to determine a probability of success. A Monte Carlo simulation is used in financial applications to better understand risk when some variables are random. In this example we are analyzing a financial plan with one variable that can be considered random – the portfolio's annual return, and one output – the value of the portfolio at the end of the plan. Any scenario in which the portfolio value is not depleted would be a success. Under one scenario, using the expected return of the portfolio, we may find the plan satisfies. But if we shock the portfolio return thousands of times using the expected return and volatility around it to generate the sample and combine that with the unchanging retirement spending and income assumptions, we create alternative possible scenarios.[7]

All of these potential outcomes are ranked in order from worst to best, and we can use this information to judge how likely our financial plan is to being realized. For example, let's assume we find a retirement lifestyle spending to be $150,000 using the expected return of the portfolio. Though it is the average result (the 50th percentile) it means there is a 50% chance it will also be *less* than $150,000. Many practitioners manage the financial plan to a more conservative level, perhaps to the 20th percentile of outcomes. That would ensure there is an 80% chance the client would be satisfied even if the portfolio underperforms its expected return. Monte Carlo simulation can derive what that 20th percentile value is. The financial advisor may find that at the 20th percentile the portfolio could only support a $100,000 annual lifestyle. If that is acceptable to the client then it is possible to proceed with the plan. If not, adjustments need to be made.

When building a portfolio, though not consciously, wealth managers are essentially using financial assets to manipulate the shape of the distribution of returns for clients. Higher returning assets (with associated higher risk) may increase the average rate of spending the portfolio can handle, but at the cost of creating a higher likelihood of bad results. For example, a client is debating between an annuity with a guaranteed minimum income payment and a mutual fund. Both have similar investment objectives and styles, but the annuity has higher embedded costs and the principal will never outperform. While this underperformance may lead one to prefer the mutual fund, it may not be the optimum choice. If the client is more concerned about having a minimum amount to spend, no matter their longevity, the annuity *may* be a better choice. The client may be willing to accept less retirement spending ability to achieve a better worst case scenario. When looking at the distribution of returns the annuity shifts the distribution to the left (lower annual spending ability), but it also creates a minimum spending ability.

---

[7] Monte Carlo Simulation would also model the correlations between each of the random variables. Though here we discuss expected portfolio return as the only random variable, in practice each component of the expected return would be a separate random variable with its own expected return, volatility, and correlation to other assets in the plan.

The example below shows annual sustainable spending ability on the x-axis and probability of that outcome on the y-axis. The baseline in dark gray (no annuity) shows the average spending ability is $150,000. Investing in the annuity (light gray columns) reduces that baseline to $110,000, but imposes a minimum payout of $60,000, eliminating much of the left tail. The advisor must evaluate how much it costs in spending ability to guarantee income regardless of longevity. Answering this question with precision would be difficult without some financial modeling program that included Monte Carlo Simulation.

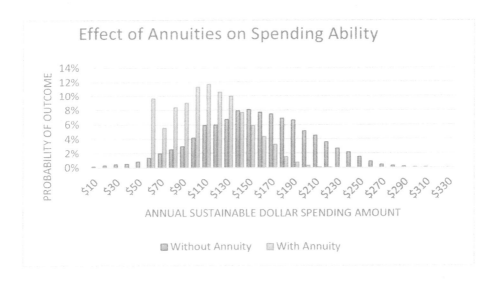

A financial advisor tweeted this derisive view of Monte Carlo Simulation: "Using past data on markets to simulate future returns just to show clients a confusing but colorful chart that implies your advice will lead to a 10% chance they'll be eating dog food and living under a bridge." Although this tweet is completely true it largely misses the point. Yes, we do use historic returns to think about the future. Financial professionals always do that. Yes, there is always a possibility the financial markets may crater just when you will rely on your assets for living expenses. But the benefit of seeing the probabilities is knowing that we can make meaningful choices in advance if the odds are not in our favor, and knowing what is in our power to control before it becomes too late.

It is important to reiterate here the importance of buy-in from the client. If a plan requires a client to take more risk than he could tolerate, the plan is infeasible. Many broker questionnaires begin with asking a client about their risk tolerance. But when a financial plan is presented the client may have a different view. A risk averse investor may be distressed if they do not have enough savings generated to maintain their lifestyle in retirement. Or, a risk tolerant investor may blanche if he sees it is possible for his portfolio to fall by hundreds of thousands of dollars. A detailed conversation with the client about the financial plan will tease out not just what is possible financially, but what can be tolerated emotionally.

Let us imagine two twin brothers, both 50 years old and each inherit ten million dollars. They both currently reside in relatively inexpensive Memphis, TN.

One brother moves to Newport Beach, California. His modest $3 million home has a large mortgage. He enjoys travel and fine food, and expects to maintain his lifestyle as long as he can. He expects to spend $350,000 per year plus $120,000 for his mortgage over the next 30 years. The other brother stays in Memphis. The mansion he buys cost a million dollars with an annual mortgage of $40,000. He has modest tastes and expects to spend $150,000 per year. They both intend to retire immediately. The brothers may have a similar portfolio and age, but their long term investment objectives and needs are quite different.

To sustain a more affluent lifestyle, the gentleman in Newport Beach may need to invest a higher percentage in stocks. A portfolio filled with bonds may succeed in getting him through his lifetime with a modest spending budget, but to fulfill his desired lifestyle, a generous allocation to stocks is absolutely necessary. Though stocks are riskier, he has a long horizon to recoup from short term losses and he is willing to take that risk. But the success of the financial plan may be extremely sensitive to the realized return on the investment portfolio. A couple of bad years at the beginning of retirement could raise the probability that there will be insufficient funds, while not investing in high return (and high risk) assets will guarantee the desired lifestyle is unattainable.

On the other hand, the gentlemen in Memphis has barely any need to be aggressive. He needs to earn a 2% return on his inheritance to maintain his lifestyle. His portfolio could be dominated by safer bonds, and as such his risk would be substantially lower.

These two individuals start out the same, but their choices and their risk tolerance direct the portfolio to be allocated very differently. In a less outlandish example, a young child's 529 plan[8] may be invested more aggressively because the funds

---

[8] A 529 plan is a tax-advantaged plan named from the underlying section of the US Tax Code from which it was created. Section 529 permits an individual to open an account to be used for primary or secondary education with investment earnings free of tax.

need not be touched for many years, and needs to keep up with expected tuition inflation. But a family's taxable brokerage accounts may be kept more conservative in case funds are needed in the near future.

This discussion has been a simple analysis using only equity and fixed income allocation, but the plan can be more elaborate, including real estate and alternative assets with their own expected returns, volatilities, and correlations with the other asset classes. We can also include appreciation of the primary residence as a source of income if a client expects to downsize in the future.

Through an iterative process, a wealth manager develops the asset allocation with the financial plan to ensure it meets the needs of the client, taking as much risk as needed to achieve goals, without needlessly exposing the client to more than is necessary.

To be sure, the resultant allocation is not deterministic. If the client is uncomfortable with the necessary risk to achieve those goals, then the goals must change if the risk can't. Conversely, if the client has the tolerance and financial resilience to absorb short term volatility then a more aggressive stance can be accommodated. Perhaps the most important characteristic of creating the financial plan is a healthy conversation, during which financial advisor and client can come to an understanding of what each can help deliver to maintain a successful, long term relationship. The allocation decision is just one result, but an important one.

A feasible financial plan requires a commitment from the client and the advisor. Hopefully, the client understands that spending too much of his income now will pull resources from the future. The advisor also has a responsibility to manage the portfolio according to how he represented it would look. As we shall see, it's less clear than it sounds.

This now-determined allocation is the *benchmark* the portfolio manager must track towards. Deviations from this benchmark could make it harder for the client to reach objectives. As noted, the financial plan is the handshake between wealth management and portfolio management. With the plan in place and a desired risk asset allocation decided, the process of portfolio construction can begin.

PART TWO: PORTFOLIO THEORY
PORTFOLIO DEFINITION

Defining what a portfolio is might seem like a silly exercise. Many readers would be satisfied thinking that a portfolio is nothing more than a collection of investments, primarily stocks and bonds, that is used to generate a return. I find that definition inadequate for two reasons:

- it may give you the sense that once you've bought the positions the portfolio is necessarily complete
- it does not prepare you for understanding the risks you actually own.

Benjamin Graham wrote "The essence of investment management is the management of risks, not the management of returns." I would adapt that definition to the portfolio. At the risk of sounding academic and out of touch with "the real world" I define an investment portfolio as a **collection of compensated risks**. After describing my definition I was told "That's silly. At the end of the day you own stocks and bonds." From an investment standpoint, that is an inadequate description of a portfolio. And from a factual standpoint, even when you think your portfolio could be so easily defined, it might be wrong.

One example of the inadequacies of saying you have a portfolio of "stocks" is that such a statement may obscure the nature of your risks. If your portfolio was a diversified basket of US large capitalization companies, then saying you have a portfolio of "stocks" is certainly adequate. This specific situation clearly does not describe the vast majority of managed portfolios though.

Consider a situation in which an advisor follows a high dividend strategy in which a large block of the portfolio is allocated into Exxon, Chevron, and Occidental Petroleum. Is the risk the same market risk as that of every other investor, or is the risk dominated by energy prices? Certainly, these risks must be different. In this case, the character of the chosen equities is more relevant than the asset class. But if one's definition of a portfolio is fixated on the asset class (e.g. stocks) and is indifferent to the risk (e.g. volatility of energy prices) then it limits the ability to understand, and hence direct, the portfolio.

Another limitation of the "Equity" label is the broader methods of accessing the markets we have through derivatives. Is owning a futures contract on the S&P

500 a stock or bond? Consider a mutual fund that uses futures and swaps (which require a minimal initial payment) to replicate a particular equity index, and then used the cash to invest in high yielding fixed income credit securities - is it a stock or a bond? Similarly, market-linked notes create limited equity-like performance, even though the instrument owned is actually a debt obligation of the issuer.   If the viewpoint of a portfolio is limited to the asset class, you may not properly understand the risks you face.

During the portfolio construction process, we must use definitions that help us move forward. If I use the definition that "a portfolio is a collection of stocks and bonds" how will I know where I am in the process? Using the definition that "a portfolio is a collection of compensated risks" forces the following questions: "What risks am I taking at any one point in time?" **and** "How much am I being compensated for these risks?"   Such dialogue dovetails well with modern portfolio theory, to be discussed later.

Before beginning construction of the portfolio we must be able to clearly articulate the portfolio objective. For institutional investment managers, their mandate is simple – outperform the benchmark. Within a wealth management context the mandate is not as straightforward. Each client is different – ages, income, risk tolerance, liquidity needs. The portfolio needs to be constructed with certain parameters built into the foundation.

The **goal** in any portfolio may be to maximize returns. Now some clients may say, "well I just want to earn a little bit; I don't need to make a lot." In reality this means "take very little risk" not "earn as little as possible." For instance, if you were able to invest two CD accounts with different banks, all else being equal, with one account paying .5% and the other paying .75%, would you be indifferent between the two? Probably not.

A portfolio manager should focus on one goal, as it directs the process coherently. For example, if a client indicates a need for both the highest return **and** the highest dividend yield, one decision could be a trade-off against the other and neither goal given priority.

Instead we build the portfolio with *constraints* in mind. A constraint does a better job of framing conditions that must be met and allows the goal to be sought without sacrificing mandatory attributes. A portfolio may be constrained to throw off 4% from income, but the client is indifferent if it is any higher. There is no utility in trying to get more and the portfolio manager can focus his attention on maximizing returns given his universe of high yielding securities.

Anything can be a constraint – but for most portfolios we should always consider Income, Liquidity, and Volatility.[9] Income may not be important for all, but it is particularly important for retired clients who want to maintain their lifestyle. A client may have expectations about when principal withdrawal will begin, or how much immediate needs are, or an expected large purchase in five-years time.

---

[9] Other constraints may include more subjective considerations like ESG restrictions, which refers to Environment, Social and Governance. Constraints of this nature restrict investments with a morally problematic nature from entering the portfolio.

Finally a client may not have the risk appetite to accept the highest returning assets, but can be accommodated with more diversification or alternative assets (which may sacrifice liquidity). Some constraints can be easily accommodated within an advisor's model. Others require more thoughtful accommodations.

Constraints help us determine the universe of securities from which to choose. If a client anticipated selling his entire portfolio to purchase a private jet, then an illiquid investment like private equity would be excluded given the inability to reclaim principal on demand. If a client needed cash for a down payment on a home, then a short-term money market fund may be included that would be inappropriate for other clients. Functionally, this should be obvious. But incorporating a constraint as a construction element, as opposed to a specific problem to solve, creates a more balanced whole.

Let's say there is a yield constraint (ie, the portfolio must generate a certain percentage in income.) Consider a portfolio that needs 4% of income earned on the principal each year. We could use a standard model equity portfolio used for many clients, and then add on very high yielding (and risky) assets to average up the yield, or we could build from the ground up an intelligent portfolio that is conscious at conception of its expectations. If higher dividend stocks are added, what characteristics will the portfolio have less of? If more high yield bonds are added, how much more risk does the portfolio have? A constraint should not subvert other characteristics managers think a portfolio must have. Taking more control of portfolio choices allows managers more levers to maximize returns, but also to minimize surprises.

Thinking about risk can be a matter of perspective. That sounds coy but clearly clients think about the risks in their portfolio differently than advisors. Clients need that portfolio to perform, and over a long horizon the absolute return is expected to be positive, otherwise those assets put away for the future would be worth less than at initiation.

Conversely, the advisor has risk from *relative* return. If the broader equity market has had a 20% gain, but the portfolio managed by the advisor is only up 10%, he needs to be able to explain the underperformance. After many periods of underperforming, the advisor begins to worry about losing clients, and has difficulty bringing on new ones. He has career risk. But there are many ways to talk about risk, and then of course there is the academic approach.

The client has risks that do not appear to be related to the portfolio, but eventually they are. For example, inflation, or purchasing power risk. Even if a client kept to a plan of steady spending, if the advisor did not consider inflation, then rising price levels could prematurely deplete the portfolio. Or a portfolio that relied on bonds to deliver return may result in insufficient asset growth to accommodate the future.

One of the most visible and vicious risks is the permanent impairment of capital. When Lehman Brothers was allowed to fail because of financing problems, or when Enron collapsed beneath its fraud, the stock essentially became worthless. Two notable, envied companies no longer existed, and the equity holders were left with shares with no value, and no possibility of future value.

The permanent impairment is not a situation that you can wait out for recovery, and illustrates the dangers of single stock investing – relying on a small number of individual stocks in the portfolio. Nobody would look at that kind of loss with a glass-half full outlook. Fortunately these losses are less common. With that said, a company need not completely disappear for it to lead to a permanent relative impairment. Some companies become left behind by new technology or can't keep up with the market needs. Buying the stock of Kodak or Blackberry at their respective peak values may also impair capital, if not on an absolute basis, then relative to what could have been if invested in the broader market.

Compared to that, the risk of temporary losses due to broad market fluctuations is always present - but rarely a permanent one - for those who have the flexibility to wait. **The risk is not the market itself, but the possibility you may need to withdraw funds at a particularly low price and miss the subsequent bounce.** That circumstance would transform a market fluctuation into a permanent impairment. It is only the ability, or constitution, of the client to stay with the market through bad times that makes market mania less risky than it seems.

Academics and quantitative practitioners use the word **Volatility** as a catch-all term for the way they measure risk, which uses price movements as the primary signifier.   Investors with a long time horizon may be less concerned with academics, because every market cycle has turned back, and stocks manage to end up higher despite all the drama.   Who would have thought that the March 2020 equity market collapse resulting from worries over the Covid-19 pandemic would be followed by many indices reaching record highs later in the same year? So why is volatility meaningful as a measure of risk?   Why does portfolio theory rest its foundations on its usefulness?

At the individual asset level, volatility is a good proxy for risk because if a security price is volatile, it means investors are having a hard time evaluating the investment's prospects.   It could be volatile because it has a vast number of difficult to forecast unknowns, or extremely sensitive to a few critical factors.

Volatility is easy to calculate and not subject to manipulation like financial statements.   An analyst does not need to interpret the result or present it in context. Volatility in one sector means the same in another.   This makes it useful in portfolio theory to shorthand the discussion of risk.   Volatility in isolation may be inadequate, and the shorthand may provide a false sense of knowledge, but it does help focus conversations about portfolio management.

We can measure volatility using the standard deviation of a security's (or market's) return around the average return.   What exactly is standard deviation, and why do we use it as a metric for measuring volatility?   In statistics, the standard deviation measures the amount of dispersion in a set of values.   Without knowing exactly how any statistical relationship is distributed, we often rely on an assumption that the data will be "normally distributed" which means that much of the data will be concentrated around the mean, or average value, with fewer data points further away.[10]   The normal distribution is modeled from naturally occurring observations in science and nature.   If you combine each data point that could be included in your sample, plotting the value of the data on the

---

[10] Financial markets are known to have far more data points that fall on the "tails" of the distribution, in other words a higher probability of outlier events, than would be predicted using a normal distribution.

x-axis and the number of times it appeared against the y-axis, it would approach a bell-shaped image.

The standard deviation is a summary statistic that provides a measure of how wide the distribution of the data is. The metric "one standard deviation" gives us an idea of how much the data is dispersed around the average. For example, if we had a classroom of first graders and were measuring height, the average may be close to 45 inches with very little variation from there. We would expect that our sample would have much less variability than the same analysis performed in a random New York City subway car with people of all ages and sizes represented in the data.

Based on the normal distribution, about 68% of the time a data point will be less than one standard deviation away from the average (34% higher and 34% lower), and 32% of the time it will be higher than one standard deviation away from average (about 16% higher and 16% lower). Using a standard deviation we can describe the scope of plausible scenarios.[11]

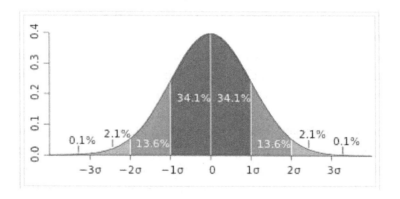

Source: Wikipedia

---

[11] Unfortunately, finance is not as ordered as nature and assuming too much precision for the probability of unlikely scenarios has led to disasters at many hedge funds. Statistics do not offer us certainty – sometimes extremely unlikely events happen. We can have more confidence discussing the averages and apply that to our analysis with some comfort, but dismissing the probability of outlier events can be very dangerous for a portfolio.

We can use this concept of standard deviation to describe the volatility in the context of investment markets and portfolios. For example, if an equity market has an average return of 8% and a volatility of 16%, we can expect returns to generally range from -8% (one standard deviation below the mean) to 24% (one standard deviation above the mean). 68% of the time returns would be in this range, but there is some probability returns will be higher or lower. Using average returns and volatility (as measured by standard deviation) we have more than two just summary statistics, we have a picture of what could happen. As you would expect, low distribution in the returns of financial assets is a good thing. The more we can rely on performance the more faith we can have in our financial plan. Typically, however, higher returns are often accompanied by higher volatility of returns.

It should be noted that *volatility can be considered good!* Exceptional returns do not occur in securities that don't have risk. The healthy returns we receive in stocks are compensation for the volatility and uncertainty we absorb. But this is also a check on reasonableness – if a security has on average returned 3% with a range of -4% and +10% it clearly would not be worth consideration if a bond could be purchased yielding 2.5% and no volatility at all.

Though volatility may be an inadequate proxy for risk as it relates to a probability of permanent loss, we find that easily quantifiable metrics enables us to get further in asking and answering questions about portfolios, and has become an integral part of modern portfolio theory. As we will discuss, the properties of a *portfolio's* volatility drive the advantage of diversification.

The adequacy of volatility as a measure of risk can certainly be debated, as it would surely not have protected investors from an investment in Enron, Lehman Brothers, Sunbeam or any other casualty of fraud, mismanagement, or strategic misses – while a comprehensive review of financial statements may have sounded an alert. Long horizon investors may be indifferent to short term drama.

The simplifying assumptions we make in portfolio theory allow us to look beyond one company's Form 10-K[12] report in creating a cohesive, powerful whole. These

---

[12] A Form 10-K is an annual report mandated by the US Securities and Exchange Commission (SEC) provides a review of a company's financial performance using standardized accounting rules.

assumptions can allow us to evaluate one investment relative to another and study the marginal impact of a portfolio change. Even long-horizon investors can agree that less risk is better than more, if expected returns are the same.

The volatility as risk concept is extremely useful but its limitations should not be ignored. For fundamental investors[13] it is a cursory metric that does not replace skilled analysis of financial statements. Meanwhile, retail clients with long horizons may be less sensitive to short term volatility. Large-capitalization US stocks have had a historical annualized return of 8%, but the annualized standard deviation of that return has been an uncomfortable 18%. However, if we use the geometric mean [14] annual return over rolling 5-year periods, the standard deviation is only 8%, as bad years are often followed by very good years, flattening the investment experience[15].

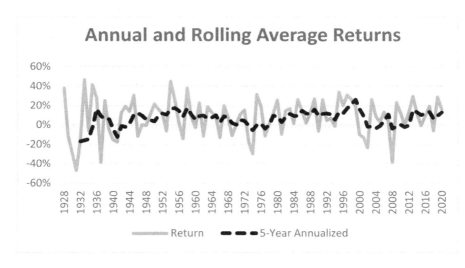

Annual and Rolling Average Returns

Source: www.macrotrends.net

---

[13] Fundamental investors concentrate on the underlying attributes of a company's stock
[14] The geometric mean differs from the arithmetic mean because it adjusts for the effects of compounding on investment returns
[15] For example, we consider the S&P 500 from 1926 – 2020. The first five year period is 1928 – 1932, the second five year period is 1929 – 1933, etc. We calculate the annualized returns of each of these five year periods and then compute the standard deviation of the data series.

If each year's experience was independent of the prior year's returns we would be much more concerned, but the tendency for the market to over-react and then "snap back" protects long term Investors who are able to hold on through the short term stock market drama. Investors should use the concept (and time horizon) of risk that is meaningful relative to their involvement in the financial markets.

Going forward I will be equating risk with volatility, as it provides us with a consistent measure of uncertainty, and a "cost" that can be compared to return. More equity exposure will generally be riskier than less. Bonds that are correlated to stocks are riskier than bonds that are not. These are some foundational concepts that may be in some ways dissatisfying, but help us build towards bigger ideas.

We have already used the term **"expected return"**, which seems anodyne but carries a statistical meaning, rather than a forecast. An expected return can refer to an analysis of historical experience of investment performance to derive an average return. It can also mean a weighted average return given discrete scenarios. We can examine a time series and believe that a certain asset class will continue to deliver similar performance in the future, *on average*. The expected return is not a forecast for any given year, it is an expectation generally for future returns, over time, given experience, or a pricing model derived result. Expected Return is part of the lexicon that practitioners of portfolio management understand and use. Its meaning, its nuance, and its context is just part of the language.

There is something elitist and offputting about the way experts in their field can talk. Their use of foreign sounding words can be exclusionary. Investment professionals are no different, and may be even worse than other professions because the language barrier can seem deliberate. Some financial professionals can use complexity as a shield from oversight, or a weapon to discourage challenges. Even well-meaning professionals have difficulty communicating with those who haven't been brought into the "club".

So how does this apply to us? When we use terms like beta, volatility, alpha, attribution, and tracking error, we are trying to explain how we think markets should react, or given what we've observed, this is how we interpret the results.

It's safe to say we do not think bonds will be as volatile as stocks, can we agree on that? Well, mostly. But having agreed on the terms stocks, bonds, and volatility, we can have that conversation. You might disagree about generalizing assumptions and point out times when experience diverged from expectations. And we can talk about how much diversification benefits a global bond portfolio. But without agreeing on the language, having a discussion can be challenging. If we found a bond that was more volatile than stocks (high yield bonds, structured debt with embedded derivatives, interest only mortgage strips), we can discuss how much more volatile they might be, or why it has more risk, or how the nature of this risk was correlated to other portfolio exposures.

Similarly, when performing research, how do we know what is good or bad? Without our jargon we would have a ruler with no lines on it. If during the same time period a stock's price doubled while another stock's price was up only 40%, how would we compare the performance without being able to quantify, in some way, how risky each investment was relative to each other?

As we become more capable of using this language, we can use it to broaden our tool kit as an investor. Adding lightly regulated and often opaque hedge funds to a client's portfolio is premature if you don't understand what the manager is doing. He may bludgeon you with words like "bespoke, portable alpha, capital structure arbitrage". How can you evaluate performance if you don't know what risks were being taken? If you don't understand the risks how do you know if it fits within a client's account? If you can't speak the language where would you begin? Unfortunately, many professionals don't have enough respect for the jargon and charge forward into complexity without the knowledge to protect them.

The words we use to build up this world help us ask questions. They help us understand what we're looking at. They help us think about what *could* happen. Without them the financial markets would just be some wild animal that we can marvel, but trying to ride would be much more harrowing. This doesn't mean we can excuse away an inability to communicate, but advisors should do their best to understand the language of a particular concept, and be able to translate in a way that resonates with clients.

This section is an apology for what comes next. No calculators are required but we will be talking about mathematical ideas. Hopefully, after wading through the more arcane theories, you can see your portfolio as more than a bunch of funds you bought. What is important is that though this theory can be unwieldy, and practical replication stymied by data that refuses to divulge clear direction, it is relevant for how we think about portfolio construction.

The next few sections discuss the groundbreaking theories introduced decades ago, as academics attempted to explain market behavior. Many of the basic assumptions are still taught in undergraduate economics classes and graduate business school classes. We do not need to be literal disciples of ancient theory, but its implications should guide some of your assumptions and how you approach portfolios. Unfortunately these theories are often taught outside the context of the real world which robs these theories of tactile relevance.

An early theory of the markets is that they follow a so-called Random Walk. This theory is borrowed from mathematics and accepts the unpredictable nature of stock prices. This theory suggests that *in the short* term stocks move in a random fashion and efforts to predict direction will fail. Over the long term, an asset's expected return will cause the price to drift higher. Today's profit forecast that must be discounted is tomorrow's realized retained earnings, and stocks will accrete towards that. But on any given day, prices are dictated by supply and demand – a large pension fund reallocating portfolios met by tepid demand of buyers, an overall bad mood in the market shoved around by political rhetoric, an influential reddit post causes temporary mayhem – there is no forecastable rhythm to the day-to-day factors that push prices around. A down move today can as easily be followed by a down mood tomorrow. Or an up move.

We default to a view of the markets that they are efficient, eventually. The Efficient Markets Hypothesis is a core assumption in modern portfolio theory. The hypothesis states that all available information about an asset is *already* reflected in its price. Later research differentiated three different forms of efficiency: weak, semi-strong, and strong form. Weak form suggests that historical prices cannot predict future prices (think technical trading strategies). Semi-strong form suggests all public information is reflected in asset prices. Strong form concludes all public and private information is incorporated.

Efficient markets theory is comfortable in some ways. For one, it reflects the reality that it is very difficult to beat the markets. If the markets were inefficient, stock pickers would have much more success. In fact, decades of experience have shown that active managers are unlikely to outperform. Efficient markets also support our view of the markets as responsive to information. From an academic standpoint, we rely on the markets to push prices of competing assets to reflect their relative risk. Immediate recalibration enables us to make simplifying assumptions that lead into modern portfolio theory.

The contradiction is that efficient markets implicitly assumes there are research folks out there with knowledge, who inform the traders making these arbitrage trades that push prices towards efficiency. It implies that research actually matters, it's just that it's difficult when so many people are doing the research. Conversely, small stocks that nobody knows about suddenly explode when they've discovered or created the next new thing. They didn't make that discovery in one day, it had been after years of effort, but the market made the decision it was important. Does this disprove efficient markets? Do massive financial or tech bubbles make it unlikely markets are efficient?

In truth, financial professionals have used efficient markets theory as a crutch. We've expected that *somebody* has to be doing the research, so the prices must be appropriate. "These risky mortgages surely have been vetted for accurate documentation. This expensive tech stock must have a great business plan." That's not necessarily true, however. When we say that markets are efficient, we should have in our mind that information moves fast, and we're probably not the first person to think that Amazon will be a great company. And yet, we still might be the first person to read a prospectus.

Efficient markets theory helps us understand relationships. The Price-to-Earnings Ratio[16], or "P/E" ratio of Coca-Cola should be in line with the P/E ratio of Pepsi because they face similar economics and markets. Or we can say that the expected return of two stocks may differ based on different exposures to market risk, company size, quantified expressions of value, or any attribute that a pricing model may discover as additive in explaining asset returns.

Let's be clear, however, that when a financial strategist says the market is forecasting something, that is an expansive view of efficient markets at work. The market doesn't know the future, it just represents the weighted average

---

[16] The P/E ratio of a stock is calculated by dividing the current market price (i.e. price per share) by the Earnings Per Share (EPS) of that company. EPS can be either reported trailing twelve months' earnings (found on the company's Income Statement) or forward looking earnings estimated by analysts.

collective beliefs of its participants. You can argue that if market participants disagreed with current asset pricing, enough of them could act to buy or sell, moving market prices to better reflect their view of the future and eventually forcing the market to a level that could imply a collective forecast. In a frictionless, liquid, perfectly informed state of affairs with no secondary interests in trading and no taxes this could be true. But reality is rarely pure enough to describe market pricing as an unbiased forecast.

This handbook is not meant to summarize decades of academic research, derive the math, or explain every nuance embedded in these theories. It is simply meant to introduce the concepts and explain how they have practical applications in your thought process. Further exploration is encouraged. The formulas here are not meant to scare, intimidate, or prescribe a method of portfolio construction. For some the math may be helpful to see.

Modern Portfolio Theory (MPT) was articulated in 1952 by economist Harry Markowitz. The framework he presented explained that the investors goal is to either maximize return for a given amount of risk, or minimize risk for a targeted expected return. As discussed before, portfolio volatility is an acceptable proxy for risk and represented by the standard deviation.

The expected return of the portfolio can be calculated as the expected return of each asset times its weight in the portfolio. If we were discussing a 60% stocks, 40% bond portfolio, and assuming stocks would return 8% and bonds would return 2%, the expected return of the portfolio would be 5.6%. Mathematically this could be expressed as:

$$E(R_p) = \sum_i w_i \, E(R_i)$$

where R_p is portfolio return, R_i is return of asset i and w_i is the weight of asset i.

One should note that if we knew what the return was going to be, why don't we just invest in the asset with the highest return? The answer is, we *don't* know what the return will be, we just have an expectation that it will likely be a certain value, based on history or a more complex valuation model. We also assume there is some probability of being higher or lower, as estimated by the volatility. While 8% may be the *expected* return for stocks, in any given year it could be +24% or -8% with equal probability, assuming a symmetrical distribution of returns.

When deriving the volatility of the portfolio we begin by calculating the variance, which is the standard deviation squared. The critical observation in MPT is the volatility of the entire portfolio is not the weighted average volatility of each component, but also incorporates the correlation[17] of each asset with every other asset in the portfolio.

The generalized variance formula is much more complicated:

$$\sigma_p^2 = \sum_i w_i^2 \sigma_i^2 + \sum_i \sum_{j \neq i} w_i w_j \sigma_i \sigma_j \rho_{ij},$$

This is definitely a lot to unpack. The first term sums the square of the weight (w_i^2) times the asset's variance (σ^2). That term alone would result in a portfolio volatility that is less than the weighted volatility of its components. The second term calculates the impact of correlations between assets. P is the symbol for correlation. Extending just the second term into math for a three asset portfolio (assets A, B and C in this notation) looks like this:

$$2w_A w_B \sigma_A \sigma_B \rho_{AB} + 2w_A w_C \sigma_A \sigma_C \rho_{AC} + 2w_B w_C \sigma_B \sigma_C \rho_{BC}$$

Four observations:

1. If correlations between all assets were zero, each term above would become zero
2. If correlations were all +1 the portfolio volatility would equal the weighted average volatility of each asset in the portfolio
3. If correlations are negative, these terms become negative and portfolio volatility *decreases*

---

[17] Correlation is a standardized measure of how much two data series, in this case financial asset returns, move with each other. It is scaled between 1 (perfect correlation) and -1 (perfect negative correlation) with 0 indicating no relationship (no co-movement) between the two data sets.

4. Adding more securities progressively complicates the formula because the correlation of every investment in the portfolio is calculated against *every other asset!*

Let's use an example. Assume two assets, split 50/50 in a portfolio. Both have a standard deviation of 12%, and we will only vary the correlation.

If correlation equals zero, we only use the first term:

$$Variance = .5^2 * .12^2 + .5^2 * .12^2 = .0072$$

Since variance is the square of standard deviation, we calculate Standard Deviation by taking the square root of the variance.

$$Standard\ deviation = 8.5\%$$

Note that this is less than the standard deviation of its components

Now let's use a correlation of +1:

$$Variance = .5^2 * .12^2 + .5^2 * .12^2 + 2*.5*.5*.12*.12*1 = .0144$$

$$Standard\ deviation = 12\%$$

Note that equals the standard deviation of the components

Finally, a correlation of -1:

$$Variance = .5^2 * .12^2 + .5^2 * .12^2 + 2*.5*.5*.12*.12*-1 = 0$$

$$Standard\ deviation = 0$$

The second part of the equation completely offsets the first

This is the heart of the diversification argument. It is only under the most extraordinary circumstances that a portfolio will have as much volatility as the weighted sum of its components. Adding additional assets, even if they have the same volatility, can still incrementally decrease overall risk. This is why diversification is called the only free lunch – it costs essentially nothing to add more stocks to a portfolio and reduces volatility, a valuable characteristic, without necessarily reducing returns.

The second crucial takeaway here is that when looking at adding additional assets to the portfolio, the relevant question is not the risk of the asset, but the correlation of that asset's performance with the rest of the portfolio. If one could create an asset with an expected return of 8%, and another that was perfectly negatively correlated that also returned 8%, regardless of each individual asset's volatility the package would guarantee an 8% return. An impossible construct to be sure, but this is the power of negative correlations between assets.

Let's examine a three asset universe with the following attributes:

	A	B	C
Return	7.5%	4.0%	6.0%
Volatility	14%	8%	11%
Correlation:			
A and B	30%		
A and C	50%		
B and C	20%		

Given this information, we can explore different portfolios and observe their calculated expected return and volatility. What happens if the allocation is split evenly between the three? We can calculate the expected return would be 5.8% and the volatility would be 8%. Is this the best we can do? It is just one possibility. Plotting out a few hundred possibilities teases out what the distribution of outcomes looks like:

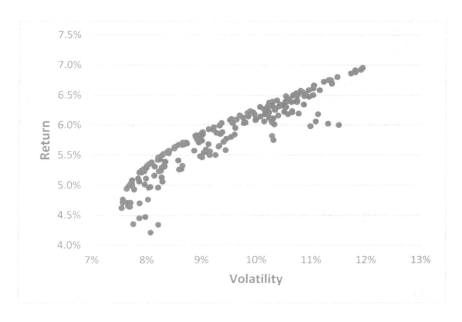

Graphically, we have a scatter plot of portfolio options. Each dot above represents a return and volatility combination derived when you combine the three different assets in different proportions. The x-axis denotes volatility, while the y-axis measures return. If we were to target a volatility, we can find the portfolio that maximizes return. Or we can choose a return bogey, and find the portfolio that minimizes volatility. This is sometimes referred to as **mean variance optimization.**

We are looking specifically at the top of the curve, that shows the optimal portfolios. The higher you go in the graph, the more return you earn for a given level of risk. This is the **efficient frontier.** Because of the advantages of diversification, the efficient frontier will generally consist of a *portfolio* of investments rather than single assets. That said, the only way to achieve the highest return is to invest only in the highest returning asset, at the cost of its volatility.

With modern computing power and data resources we do not need to constrain our investigation to a universe of three assets. We can look at granular breakdowns of global stock markets (small/mid/large cap, value/growth, etc) as well as broad categories of fixed income and alternatives like real estate and private equity. We can include as much historical data as we can find. An excellent resource to examine efficient frontiers and asset correlations can be found at www.portfoliovisualizer.com

In practice, efficient frontiers are susceptible to picking out and overweighting historical winners that do not reflect current valuations or future realities. Over the last ten years, US Large Capitalization Growth stocks have been a dominant performing asset class, while US Value stocks (of all capitalization sizes) have had a most difficult decade. An efficient frontier created using this period as a baseline would prescribe portfolios that are lopsided, overweighting the best performers and pushing only small allocations to others. Volatility and correlations are a little more stable than returns but also subject to drift. Most distressingly correlation tends to increase during times of stress, when you are most dependent on their diversification benefits!

An over-reliance on suspect historical data is an obvious fault of this analysis, but it need not be taken literally. There is no necessity that historical performance is the only guide for relative future returns either. Even if the US equity indexes have historically outperformed global indices (those outside the US), an investor should not automatically assume that the expected return of US stocks will always be higher than those outside the US. Practitioners can incorporate their own estimates of returns based on comparative valuation.

Sophisticated pricing models are sometimes used to adjust or create future expected returns. Using fundamental market inputs fed into a model can differentiate markets. Quantitative investment portfolio researchers use a field of mathematics called Robust Optimization to evaluate portfolios given **uncertainty** and **variability** in the return expectations. These models can solve for portfolio allocations that are less driven by single estimates of return that can be far off the mark. The resultant portfolios may be more diversified and have less exposure to extreme outcomes because they are less dependent on static inputs that could be very wrong.

The efficient frontier helps us think about our goals as portfolio managers. We are not trying to take risk for the sake of risk. We are trying to evaluate how we can best be compensated for the risks we are taking. Whether your approach is formalized with explicit assumptions or more casual, you should recognize the tradeoff and have some method to evaluate your overall portfolio exposures.

The efficient frontier shows the option set of portfolios with risky attributes. Each asset presents some risk, there is no option for an investor to achieve zero risk unless assets happen to be negatively correlated with another.

In reality, risk free (zero volatility) assets do exist, such as US Treasury Bills. It creates an interesting new option with respect to the efficient frontier. On one hand, if we chose to have a completely risk-free portfolio, we can choose only the risk-free asset and earn the rate (return) provided by that asset. Alternatively, we can choose a combination of the risk-free asset, and any portfolio on the efficient frontier. But which portfolio?

Our goal is to maximize return for a unit of risk. We know the marginal return one earns for incrementally more risk gets smaller and smaller. Doubling the amount of risk you take does not double the amount of return, theory suggests, and it makes intuitive sense. At first, the fruits of diversification give you incrementally more return without taking much more risk, but only for so long.

The ideal portfolio we are looking for is at the point where we've maximized the amount of incremental return we can achieve per additional unit of risk. This is called the tangency portfolio. If we draw a straight line from the risk-free return on the y axis to the tangency portfolio, we have what is called the **Capital Market Line**.

Now, instead of choosing any of the superior options along the frontier, we can create a portfolio from only two choices: an optimal non-zero risk portfolio and the risk-free asset. Note that we can choose as much or as little of the non-zero-risk portfolio as we like. If we want to lower volatility we add proportionately more of the risk-free asset to the portfolio. If we are already fully invested in the optimal risk portfolio and want to further increase return, we can (theoretically) use leverage to increase exposure to the optimal portfolio. **This Capital Market Line becomes the new efficient frontier.**

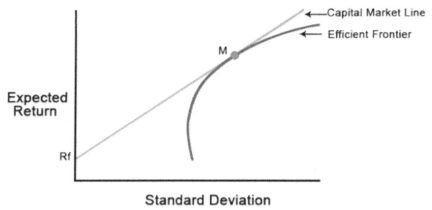

Source: https://www.wallstreetmojo.com/capital-market-line/

Because this risky portfolio is efficient, it is an appropriate allocation for all investors, regardless of their risk tolerance. I've heard advisors say "for more risk tolerant clients I invest in international stocks" or something similar that seems incrementally more risky. But does that make sense? The question is not "is this asset attractive"? The question is "does this asset, in combination with the rest of my portfolio, increase my expected return, or decrease my risk?" In that sense, if an asset achieves one or the other, it should be in *every* client's portfolio. **Our tool to control risk is the allocation to the risk free asset, not the composition of the risky portfolio.**

Over many years before 2021, growth stocks had dominant returns. While examining a prospective portfolio, one of my colleagues questioned why I suggested that a client's equity portfolio look the same as our other clients. "She has substantial net worth, why should we invest her like our retired clients? Why invest so heavily in value stocks, she has much more tolerance for risk?" It was a difficult conversation, it seems like growth stocks have higher upside and value is for the conservative set. And yet, historically that's completely wrong. Value stocks have delivered **higher** returns than growth stocks over the last few decades, but this is because Value stocks are perceived as *risky*, which is why their share prices are inexpensive relative to earnings. This begs the question: should every investor only buy value stocks? Of course not. Are growth stocks better

43

for aggressive investors? They may also have higher risk (you are paying much more for a dollar of earnings and eventually requires proof in performance) and at some point the likelihood of the company delivering extraordinary performance to justify its price withers.

At the end of the day, we do not know what will outperform. That is why we create diversified portfolios, and that is also why when we engage with risk, the process should theoretically be the same for any client. Because we do not know, our best approach is to minimize the volatility for the amount of return we seek, and dial the allocation to the risk portfolio (against the risk-free allocation) to adjust for client needs.

In practice, it is less straightforward. Some clients expect shorter term, tactical exposure to winning sectors. These portfolios may differ from longer term strategic baselines that are better for more conservative clients. Theories offer no guidance on how you position for short-term perceived market anomalies. It only guides towards having a consistent view for an efficient, long horizon allocation.

Academics make some more assumptions that broaden the interpretation of the Capital Market Line:

1. All investors seek to optimize mean variance in their portfolios
2. Investors can borrow and lend unlimited amounts at the risk free rate
3. All investors have identical assumptions about returns, variances, and covariances
4. All investors have the same time horizon
5. Transactions are frictionless.[18]
6. Inflation is predictable and interest rates are constant

Theoretically, if all of these assumptions hold, then **all** investors would use the same risky portfolio. In this scenario, the tangency portfolio can be considered the **market portfolio**, that must contain all stocks, and in proportion to their market value. This is because if it was not in the market portfolio, then it would not be owned by any investor and consequently, worthless. The implication of these assumptions is that the market portfolio is the most efficient portfolio you could have. These are dubious assumptions. But they are simplifying, helping us tame thousands of global investments and unify them into a describable **system**.

At this point, readers can say this is all too theoretical. Some readers would close the book and say this is worthless. John Bogle thought these concepts were meaningful and created the Vanguard family of mutual funds, which track major indices at minimal cost. It has been very difficult for active money managers to consistently beat the indexes they track, validating at least some of this theory. Indeed, active managers very rarely consistently beat their benchmarks. According to Standard & Poor's, after 5-years 75% of managers underperform the large-cap index. After 20 years that number rises to 94%.[19]

---

[18] Frictionless transactions means there are no trading costs or commissions when making portfolio changes and the investor trading activity will not impact market pricing.
[19] Standard & Poor's, Year-End 2020 SPIVA Scorecard

If you are a disciplined advisor with very few portfolio models, this concept of a single market portfolio may resonate. Many advisors, however, invest each client with the hottest, newest new idea, and the collective book of client portfolios are like unmoored boats, adrift and weighed down by investments that seemed like a good idea at the time. At present the reason and the context for how and why each client was allocated is lost, and the portfolio just moves along with few changes or direction.

Understanding this framework of keeping a single market portfolio, or your interpretation of it, helps you answer the question: **What are you trying to do?** Advisors should grip hard to their view, their understanding of the market portfolio because things happen fast – new clients, tax planning, withdrawals, loss harvesting, divorces -- with hundreds of clients the 'why' of what was happening when investments were made slips. If you always have your market viewpoint, your concept of efficient risk, you can better keep your balance.

Up to now we've been speaking theoretically about "the market". And theoretically, the market includes every investable asset. It could include commodities, art work, precious metals, and private companies. It certainly includes large caps, small caps, developed international, and emerging markets.

But as we migrate from the theoretical world to the practical process of portfolio construction, we can think of the market as portfolio options on the efficient frontier from which to choose our "risky basket", and we can use **indexes** to track what we consider to be the market.

What exactly is an index? An index can be thought of across three characteristics:

- A description of the Basket of Securities to be included: This can include asset class (e.g. stocks, bonds, real estate), sub asset-classes (e.g. Treasury Bonds, Corporate bonds), or other descriptors (e.g. Large-Cap Size for Stocks, Investment-Grade for bonds).
- A methodology for what securities are to be included, as well as how the index value is to be calculated.
- An Index Provider: This is typically a private company that "manages" and licenses the index so that external organizations can use it for publishing or research purposes.

Equity indices tend to be the most well known. In the United States, we tend to use the Standard and Poor's (S&P) 500 for broad market returns[22], and often quote the Dow Jones Industrial Average, which tracks only 30 stocks. Construction of these indexes is mostly market capitalization weighted, that is the largest companies by market capitalization have the proportionally largest representation in the index, just as theory would prescribe. That said, there are other indexes such as the Dow Jones which are price weighted; the higher *priced*

---

[22] While the S&P 500 is often cited as a metric for market return, other less well-known indexes like the Russell 3000 and Wilshire 5000 includes smaller companies as well as the largest, making them more representative of the broader market.

companies are given larger weights. For our purposes capitalization weighted provides a better representation of the market.

There are thousands of financial market indices, each with a different geographic or market segment specificity. Some are broadly defined (like the Vanguard Total Market Index) or narrow (like S&P Small Cap Growth).

Indices give us a frame of reference. If the Dow rose 1000 points, people have a concept of what that means. This by itself is not completely meaningful in the portfolio construction process. As professional investors we need to identify a **benchmark.** A benchmark can be a single index, or a combination of indices that we use as a baseline: for what we include in the portfolio, and how it should perform.

Some advisors argue that they are long term investors, and performance vs a benchmark is irrelevant to them, or their custom allocation for a client cannot be compared. But having a benchmark that you can defend as a baseline helps begin the conversation about your investment style. For example, if you communicate to a client that the S&P 500 index as your benchmark, it implies you have an affinity for big, established US companies. A benchmark helps guide your process and constrains your options. These guardrails force you to justify decisions that move you away from the "neutral". If your benchmark is a global equities index, adding hedge funds requires an evaluation, and an explanation of how it fits in. Benchmarks force you to be aware of your allocations, and when used properly help you understand your relative valuations. Perhaps above all else, the use of benchmarks makes you accountable to your clients.

A benchmark can be as basic or complex as your portfolio vision or needs. It can be as simple as the S&P 500 alone, or a broader market index definition like the MSCI All Country World Index (ACWI)[23]. It can be a bond index to replicate a lower risk profile, or it can be combined with a single equity index to accommodate what a partial bond allocation would look like.[24] It can be very complex and

---

[23] The MSCI ACWI represents large and mid-cap countries across the globe (23 developed and 27 emerging markets), approximately 85% of the capitalization in each market.

[24] The Bloomberg Barclays U.S. Aggregate Bond Index, which consists of about 10,000 individual bonds, is considered a good representation of the U.S. investment grade fixed income market. It used to be known as the Lehman Agg.

delineated, with a specific benchmark allocation to granular market segments like small cap, mid cap, large cap and international, and can include alternative asset type indices like real estate and private equity. Your benchmark helps you explain your view of the world, your vision of the efficient frontier.

If you don't use a benchmark as a guide, how will you know if you've made mistakes? How long will it take to realize you've been on the wrong path? How do you explain to your clients that you are doing what you said you were going to do, when performance looks better somewhere else? An elaborated and understood benchmark is the frame of your portfolio, and should be created thoughtfully.

Your benchmark acts as a statement of intent and your actual portfolio may look quite similar to the characteristics of the benchmark. However, your benchmark may not be perfectly suited all the time. Discretionary investment management provides the flexibility for financial advisors to judiciously manage assets. Opportunities do change, and investment portfolios can reflect that. Be cognizant that the moment you deviate from the benchmark, you are making **active** decisions, and your portfolio has **active bets**. Being "active" is not in reference to how many trades you make, but the condition of deviating from your benchmark. Note that being active may not be deliberate, even accidental differences result in an active posture.

Being active hopefully means you are using your intuition, experience, and research to enhance what you've told clients your goal was. If your benchmark is the S&P 500, and you are not invested in one of many S&P 500 index products (i.e. a **passive** portfolio), you should have reasons to believe that index is at least temporarily flawed. If you think the index is permanently flawed it may be more appropriate to select an alternative benchmark.

Being "passive" against an index is a term without flexibility. Stock indexes are easy to replicate with either mutual funds or ETFs. Owning passive sector funds with all the same stocks as an index may still create active bets if the proportions are assigned differently from the market. Our active decisions are not just which stocks to own, but the choice of sectors, market size segment, geography, and other economic factors that impact return.

Once your performance diverges from your benchmark, you now have an **active return, or alpha.** Alpha in its simplest description is the performance of the portfolio minus the performance of the benchmark during a certain period of time, sometimes referred to as a "lookback period". The lookback period could be the last quarter, year, or multiple years and would show the periodic and cumulative effect of your decisions to deviate from your benchmark.

It is the investment manager's goal to maximize alpha. That does not mean the goal is to earn the highest returns possible, rather it means high returns within the constraints of the portfolio's mandate. An ultra-short fixed income fund that consistently beats its index by 20bp has done a superb job. A fund that beats its index by 200bp is probably doing something wrong. While the calculation of alpha is easy, the interpretation of alpha may require more effort.

At the security level, interpreting alpha is more difficult. For example, how do you compare the return of a stock against the return of the bond? Clearly they have different risk characteristics, and should be judged accordingly. Investment practitioners use the term **Risk Adjusted Return** to denote a more nuanced view.

We use the Beta of a stock or portfolio as our proxy for risk. If in a given year the stock market was up 10% and the return on the risk free rate was 2%, the market outperformance would have been 8%. Any stock with a Beta of 1 would have been expected to return 10%. A stock with a Beta of 2 would have been expected to return 18%, not 20. This is because the impact of beta is calculated on the outperformance of the market over the risk free rate. We calculate alpha by subtracting the Beta times the excess return of the market (over the risk free rate) from the actual return of the asset. In formula form:

$$\alpha_i = \Delta_i - \beta_{iM}\Delta_M$$

Where α_i = risk adjusted return of asset I, Δ_i = excess return of asset I, β_{iM} = the beta of asset i with respect to the market, and Δ_M is the excess return of the market over the risk free rate.

I was looking at returns of a mutual fund in a portfolio that had underperformed its benchmark the S&P 500 index for a decade and asked the advisor who used it why he still included it in models. He responded "It has superior risk adjusted returns." Indeed, the beta was very low. And the returns were low as well. Was that the goal?

Investment managers often say they seek **"superior risk-adjusted returns"** while describing their goals. But the term has been used too broadly and without context. Many hedge funds can indeed quantify exactly how much beta they are targeting and explain their returns relative to the risk taken. Other fund managers may be implying they are conservative investors and underperformance is caused by their circumspect nature. But it should be noted that when one sees "superior risk adjusted returns" it may just be a clever way of saying poor performance.

When we build our portfolios, ideally we are trying to maximize returns for a given level of risk, or minimize risk for a targeted return. In other words, how much return is generated for a given unit of risk. As it turns out, the "tangency" or "market portfolio" where the Capital Market Line meets the Efficient Frontier occurs at the point when that ratio is highest. We call that the Sharpe Ratio after its developer Professor William Sharpe, and is another "risk adjustment" metric.

The Sharpe Ratio can be calculated as the percent return of a portfolio or asset over a period minus the return on a risk free asset during that period, divided by the standard deviation of the portfolio returns. We remove the risk free return because the volatility of that component is theoretically zero, and investors should not get credit for the component of returns which requires no skill. Your choice of risk-free rate can be a 3-month treasury bill or a 10-year note, as long as you are consistent in your choice. Sharpe Ratios are meant to present comparisons of returns against similar portfolio mandates.

In an ideal world we would take an efficient portfolio with an attractive Sharpe Ratio and use that risk component portfolio for every client risk profile. Then we would adjust our exposure to the risk-free rate to personalize a portfolio for a specific client. To achieve higher returns we would borrow money (use financial leverage) to have more exposure to risk or reduce risk by lending money through buying risk-free assets like Treasury bills.

This should sound redundant, as discussed previously with the "market portfolio". But as we move from theory to practice, we need mechanisms to understand what we are doing. When we add portfolio assets, are we improving the Sharpe Ratio? When we compare mutual fund returns, are we aware of how much risk (volatility) a manager is taking to achieve their outcome? Is a hedge fund using leverage to achieve a target when their history of generating sufficient returns is low?

Some bold investors like to say they want investments with "high risk, high reward". But we need to put boundaries around what is acceptable risk. An investment that is equally likely of doubling your money, or losing everything, has an expected return of zero and an inappropriate investment. A Sharpe Ratio either explicitly calculated or intuited gives us a framework to gauge an appropriate risk/return tradeoff.

One caveat applies when using the Sharpe Ratio for fixed-income portfolios. After long periods of good economic activity, funds with the highest amount of credit risk tend to have impressive Sharpe Ratios, as each month they earn higher interest income without experiencing much volatility. They look impressive until an economic shock pummels the fund's value compared to that boring government bond fund. This is not to say that risk in bond funds should be avoided, but you should be aware of what these numbers mean, and what drives them.

THE OPTION SET OF COMPENSATED RISK

Earlier we discussed an alternative definition of a portfolio as a set of compensated risks. This compares to the traditional breakdowns of stocks, bonds, cash, and alternatives. The problem with the traditional approach is it does not acknowledge where risk is coming from. A portfolio invested 60% in equities and 40% in US Treasurys is very different from a portfolio 60% Equities and 40% in so-called "junk bonds". A hedge fund targeting low volatility or uncorrelated returns looks different from a fund aiming for home runs. It is perhaps semantics, but recognizing risk and its sources is the first step towards controlling it.

We should concentrate on *compensated* risks. There are plenty of risks out there that do not systematically provide a reasonable and obtainable return, and we should not chase them. But innovation in the security markets has helped improve our access to risk and more diversified return. Mutual funds and ETFs are readily available, and newer "interval funds" that only offer monthly or quarterly liquidity, allow for retail investors access to illiquid investments styles.

Generally we are trying to invest in these broad categories of risk: Equity, Risk-Free Interest Rate Risk, Credit Risk, and Inflation Risk. We can access these through various combinations of stocks, bonds, hedge funds, private equity, REITs, etc.

Whether we use an asset class basis (investing based on allocations to stocks and bonds) or a risk basis (investing based on exposure to identifiable risks like market, interest rates, credit, etc) to describe our investment options, putting the frame around our choices clarifies what we can do, and should do. We are not picking assets at random, we are building a cohesive portfolio with suitable risks and acknowledged tolerances.

Why does it matter? Here is another example -- let's assume a client's fixed income allocation has a large position in corporate bonds. His financial advisor also believes that hedge funds, as an asset class, are good at diversifying risk, and invests in a fund that seeks opportunities in "structured credit." It has a very good track record, a little volatile, but impressive and appears uncorrelated to the stock market. But the corporate bond position and the hedge fund are highly correlated. You can have either, or both, but they are not separate from a risk standpoint, they are different vehicles for the same exposure.

Or a client has an unmanaged portfolio of a small number of technology stocks. The advisor ignores the assets not being managed and invests the client assets in his standard investment model, which is also overweight technology stocks. The advisor should have consulted with the client before adding more of the same risk.

As portfolio managers in the financial advisor role, if we are placing clients' assets and building portfolios, we have to know what we are doing and why we are doing it. Plugging in new investment products is not a bolt on exercise. You are creating a larger, more tangled spider web that needs to be understood. In the example above, the financial advisor may wish to replace his corporate bond exposure with secure government bonds if he wishes to add the structured credit hedge fund to the mix. This may generate a higher return without overloading the portfolio with the same type of risk.

It is easier to manage portfolios from the risk perspective. Returning to the concepts of the efficient frontier, you should ask how you can best leverage a particular risk to get the greatest return. You are in control of the risks you take. Don't let marketing and track record of an investment be your due diligence. An investment deemed attractive on its own is insufficient analysis. What is the marginal impact to *your* client's portfolio?

Being a portfolio manager is a job that could never end. There are always seemingly better ways to get where you want to go, and unfortunately good ideas begin to look better and better, and similar and similar. Risk can be a seduction – it is fun to look at complex instruments with high promised returns, and many times it is very rewarding, up until it's not. At every step it is important to consider: what trap may I have just stepped in? What risks have I exposed my clients to?

EQUITIES

When it comes to long horizon investing for client portfolios the first asset class we think of is equities. They are the workhorse of the portfolio, generating the most reliable returns *over time*. They are liquid and easily accessible. For this discussion, we are not talking about any particular stock, but broadly, an investment in the stock market – taking systematic risk, taking beta.

Over time, but not *all* the time, equities as an asset class has a solid history of impressive returns. Looking back in history from 1950 to 2020, the range of calendar year returns is from +47% to -39%. Clearly a volatile, risky asset class. But market collapses are often followed by rebounds. On a 5-yr rolling basis, the worst return was -3% per year, the best period generated +28% per year. Over rolling 20-yr periods, the *worst* performance was +6%, the best was +17%.

What this history suggests is that when given a long horizon, return volatility, our primary definition of risk, collapses. This is not to say that stocks are not risky, but when planning over long periods we should be able to relax some of our concerns.

So why do stocks have such a positive history? There are a couple of reasons. First, they are valued with risk in mind. Benjamin Graham once said "In the short run, the market is a voting machine but in the long run, it is a weighing machine." Every day, supply and demand dictate market movements. Who wants to buy it, who needs to sell it? And price changes reflect how much each party needs to make a trade.[25] During the dot-com bubble in the late 1990s through 2001, one of the reasons the market bubbled up was that everyone wanted to own a dot-com stock, but there simply weren't enough of them being created to sate the demand! But eventually it came back down to earth, because the *valuations* didn't make sense. But most of the time there is an imposed reasonableness that checks how far a stock price can climb. We can at least confidently argue that the current market value should not be higher than all the future earnings.

---

[25] The adage that prices go up when there are more buyers than sellers is often ridiculed, because there are always the same number of buyers and sellers. But in truth, prices change when there is an unmatched number of buyers and sellers *at a given price*.

At its core, professional investors' and analysts' efforts to value a stock have two aspects: 1. attempting to calculate a company's future cash flows (no easy task), and 2. *discounting* those cash flows to the present (which can be arbitrary). Discounting is the market's method of accounting (and providing compensation) for risk – taking the value of future cash flows and adjusting them to the present using our required rate of return.

How much must I be compensated to part with $100 today to possibly receive payment in the future? It doesn't matter whether we are referring to stocks or bonds. Every investment is just a promise of future compensation in return for present obligation. The less clear or specific the promise, the higher the required compensation. With bonds the promise is often clear: a coupon, a maturity, and a liquidation priority. With stocks, analysts attempt to calculate those future ownership benefits (earnings), and then decide what those promises are worth today, given an appropriate discount to ensure a risk appropriate return. The market price of the asset is the mechanism we see that combines the outlook for earnings and cash flows and an appropriate risk-determined discount rate that helps ensures satisfactory return.

In bonds this is easy to see. If the bond's coupon payment equals its required return, the bond will trade at par. But if the required return (the yield to maturity) changes, the price will change. If the market YTM increases, the bond price will fall, allowing an investor to realize the market required return regardless of the security's cash flow. There is an adage that there are no bad bonds, only bad prices. With regard to equities, as long as the market imposed an adequate concession (and wasn't too optimistic), and as those cash flow expectations are realized, stocks will realize returns as earnings are generated or dividends paid.

I've heard arguments that stocks are a Ponzi scheme, as they require another investor paying more than you paid to generate a return. The fallacy of this argument is that what a share of stock represents changes over time. Over years, companies use their profits and resources to build new factories, patent new inventions, develop better distribution and sourcing, among many other factors. Each share of stock controls more productive capability over time. Hence, while the price per share does indeed increase, so does the underlying value.

Another question is "why do stocks go up *so much?*" If economic growth averages 2-3%, why do stocks go up 8-10% per year? Part of the answer is explained above, in that we *demand* they do. We may assume revenue increases similar to economic growth but that is only part of the analytical process. A fully elaborated model of a company's expected financial performance would include estimates of all crucial parameters to capture a likely path of earnings. But those earnings would still be discounted at an appropriate rate to compensate an investor for his risk.[26] This may seem academic, but we see it in practice. Value stocks are often slow growing companies, and yet they historically have outperformed. Why? They trade at a lower Price/Earnings ratio, which means they are cheaper relative to the rest of the market.[27] The lower price relative to earnings generates the higher return we demand.

Economics certainly creates conditions for stocks to succeed, but stocks are not necessarily the economy. For example, there are about 6 million companies in the United States. Only 5500 of them are publicly traded. And yet we often pay attention to just the biggest 500 (within the S&P 500), or sometimes just 30 (in the Dow Jones Industrial Average). We are by definition looking at the outliers, growing the fastest, the largest, the most profitable. We are also looking at the future. The companies with the largest market capitalization may not have the most revenue, instead they may be the ones growing the fastest and will eventually be bigger or have the highest profit margins.

Indexes don't go to zero. They are populated with mostly profitable companies whose cashflows have been discounted. Discounting is a risk control. Owning one micro-cap company discounted using a 20% discount rate can be highly risky because these small stocks do not have the balance sheet and financial flexibility to withstand economic stress. They are also likely to be growing but have an

---

[26] An early academic model of a stock's return is called the Capital Asset Pricing Model, or CAPM. This model prescribes that the discount rate used to value a stock should be in proportion to the beta of the stock relative to the market plus the risk free fate. Higher beta stocks (riskier) would have a higher discount rate, low beta stocks a lower discount rate.

[27] This should not be interpreted to mean that every investor creates discounted cash flow analyses to determine whether they are receiving a reasonable return before investment. But like other aspects of portfolio theory, we assume there are enough market participants who are methodical in their investment approach who can drive pricing towards justifiable values. If a stock is too expensive, it is sold from portfolios driving the price down. If it is relatively cheap, it is added to portfolios. This dynamic occurs even if every investor is not actively evaluating the cash flow and return assumptions of the investment.

unproven product or service. However, owning 100 highly discounted diversified companies is much less risky than owning one, as losses in one are offset by attractive returns in others.

Stocks are built to generate returns, over time. It can be easy to overanalyze, get squeamish, and over-complicate the thought process. We don't need to incorporate noise like presidential election cycles into the asset allocation decision. There can clearly be an evaluation of whether they are too expensive but that is a *tactical* decision. When constructing portfolios and benchmarks, it is important to use them as the engine of performance, to the extent there is sufficient safe assets for near-term liquidity emergencies.

Investing in equity securities (stocks) has been relatively straightforward for the average investor ever since the first discount brokers brought inexpensive trading to the masses. Prior to their emergence, individual investors needed to go through established Wall Street firms that made hefty commissions on each trade. The idea of building a portfolio wasn't part of the plan – the information wasn't there and trading costs and limitations prohibited the precision that artful portfolio construction requires.

Now everything is simpler with free or nearly free trading, and information about portfolio positioning is more readily available. For decades the general public has had the ability to get involved, and now, if anything people can be overwhelmed by the options.

Investing in stocks can be as easy as...well... buying stocks. Robinhood will send you fireworks when you trade. There is nothing exotic now about using an app on your phone and trading. You have complete control of what you own, and can also manage the capital gain realization at your discretion. The caveat, as discussed earlier, is that it is hard to completely diversify a portfolio of individual stocks and too easy to overweight risks and lose money.

Within this century there have been enough spectacular flameouts that it should be apparent that risk is always present in portfolios of a limited number of stocks. Beside the risk aspect, there are functional difficulties building diversified portfolios of global individual stocks. How would we know and perform the due diligence on market sectors we are not familiar with? How would you be able to choose a diversified package of small cap stocks with no name recognition, or a global portfolio representing all the countries in Europe, Asia, and Latin America? It is comfortable to see the individual line items of recognizable companies in your portfolio, but there are definite limitations.

Mutual funds, as an investment vehicle, have been the solution to creating a diversified portfolio with little effort for decades. And fortunately we are seeing less capital invested in the A shares with egregious front-end loads, and overall management fees have been coming down. Every flavor is available, from active to passive, domestic and international. Funds can be ultra focused with 20 holdings or broadly diversified with thousands of stocks.

Though fees have come down there are still some disadvantages in the product. First, regardless of your holding period an investor may be subject to taxable capital gains distributions, which can be a nasty surprise in December. As long as you are an owner on the date of record, the fund can distribute gains to each investor which is a taxable event. It's not straightforward to track the pending distribution, though it is usually published on their funds' website in advance. But most investors are not thinking about taxable gains before they buy a fund.

Another problem with mutual funds is "end of day pricing" and trading. Mutual fund shares are created on demand when an investor places a buy order for shares. Investment buys and sells are netted each night and transacted at the net asset value calculated at the close of the day. This creates a market timing risk, as an investor is unable to pinpoint the price at which you execute the trade – the market can move against you from the moment you place your order through the end of the day. In volatile markets this can result in performance slippage if you trade in or out of funds against continuously priced market traded products.

Because mutual funds must keep cash on hand to satisfy redemption requests, they have a disadvantage in return as the cash holding drags down performance in a bull market. Some funds manage the cash allocation very efficiently but you still may find a large cash balance maintained for liquidity or to express a market view. Investors are paying fees on all assets, regardless of how it is invested.

Separately Managed Accounts (SMAs) are created for higher net worth investors who can meet large minimum balances. The advantage of SMAs are professional management, staffed by experienced and resourced institutional managers that often mimic a related mutual fund's mandate and strategy. The investor directly owns the individual securities that would be found in the mutual fund. This gives the investor more transparency and more control of gains realization and tax loss harvesting, often at lower fees than similarly mandated mutual funds.[28]

---

[28] Tax loss harvesting is the process of selling securities that have declined in value and buying substantially similar securities that are expected to have the same performance. This locks in tax losses that can be used to offset current or future capital gains.

Exchange traded funds, or ETFs have been one of the most exciting new investment vehicles in recent years. Originally developed in the 1990s to track indices, ETFs have steadily evolved into a go-to instrument to target many different granular investment goals. They also have the advantage of trading all day on exchanges providing real time pricing for each transaction.

Like mutual funds, ETFs package a portfolio of securities for individual investors, but the construction mechanism is different. Whereas mutual fund shares are created at the end of each day based on net inflows, ETF shares are created as needed throughout the day. When shares of an ETF are near the net asset value of the underlying stocks, the ETF shares can trade directly from a buyer to a seller on the open market. But when the market price drifts too far from the net asset value, a specialized investor called an Authorized Participant (AP) helps keep the value in check. When the ETF price is too high, the AP will collect the underlying stocks in a share of the fund and exchange them for a new share of the ETF from the sponsor to sell into the market, which will nudge the price down. Or conversely the AP can buy a share on the open market and exchange it for the individual components to push the ETF price up.

The interesting side effect of this process is that during the exchange, the ETF sponsor will deliver the shares with the lowest cost basis to the AP, maintaining the highest cost basis shares in the ETF portfolio. *This minimizes the tax impact of capital gains for investors holding the ETF.* ETFs also have the advantage of transparency. Because ETFs are exchangeable into its component securities by the AP, its individual holdings must be reported daily. This compares with minimum quarterly reporting for mutual funds.

ETFs began life targeting indexes with very low fees. As ETFs grew in popularity, the number of indexes replicated with ETF proxies exploded. Later, indexes were created at the specific request of ETF sponsors to create specific rules-based investment strategies. Some of these funds and similar mutual funds are called "smart beta" because they purport to own the market portfolio, but tilted towards attributes that seem to statistically outperform. They are passive in the sense that there is no human thumb on the scale, the rules dictate what is included and excluded, and passive against the index they were created to follow. Moreover, the lack of ongoing human intervention keeps the costs very low. But to be sure, passive to a very specific index does not mean it is passive to *your* index.

Recently, some new ETFs have completely moved beyond the index based roots and become active vehicles for stock picking and alpha generation. Some mutual fund companies are converting to ETF structures to avoid losing market share. ETFs are more efficient to trade (you know price and proceeds immediately at trade execution) and do not have market timing risk caused by end of day pricing. The trend away from mutual funds will likely continue.

Direct Indexing is a newer category of SMA, made possible by the low cost of trading shares. It seeks to mimic an existing index, fund, or portfolio model using individual stocks instead of diversified funds.[29] For relatively smaller universes like the S&P 500, the Direct Index manager can easily buy all shares and accurately replicate the index performance while retaining the ability to realize gains and losses at the individual stock level. This would matter, for example, during years of high returns in the market when owning a single ticker representing the index would present onerous tax impacts if a client needed to reduce or adjust exposure. If one owned each individual company, there would likely be some positions that would have lower or negative returns that would present less of a tax burden if liquidated, or offer a tax loss harvesting opportunity. Direct Indexing can also be useful for combining a client's legacy assets with a new advisor's investment model. The Direct Indexing approach would be able to accept more of a client's legacy assets because it could use less of none of those specific stocks (and those like it) when it replicates the advisor's new model, and over time can use losses to ease out of high gain positions. If the advisor only had the choice of mutual funds or ETFs there would be no ability to manage exposures with that precision. With Direct Indexing the advisor could efficiently combine the old portfolio with a new mandate, using a statistical optimization process to either target an accepted level of realized gains or target a satisfactory level of deviation from the advisor's model, measured by Tracking Error (to be discussed later).

---

[29] For more complex investment models that would include thousands of securities, a Direct Indexing manager would use "statistical sampling" to broadly replicate the risk profile of the model, incorporating perhaps hundreds of stocks instead of thousands.

Fixed income has many uses within a portfolio, though it is sometimes abused and misunderstood. Investors typically think of individual bonds when considering the fixed income asset class but bond funds, ETFs, CDs, and money market funds could also be included in the category.

Fixed Income is often seen as boring or staid. A "hold to maturity" instrument that grandparents gift to grandchildren. It does not typically have the wild gyrations of equities and it doesn't have the romantic narrative that a good stock story has. But fixed income tracks the macroeconomic pulse more than any other asset class. Fixed income traders are glued to their Bloomberg terminals looking out for economic data releases at 8:30am, interpreting those statistics for what they portend for economic growth, inflation, Federal Reserve Policy, and especially interest rates.

Fixed Income doesn't always mean that the income or return is actually set in stone. What it means is that the method of distributing cash flows is determined when the security is created. It could be a plain vanilla fixed coupon paying bond that matures at a set date, a callable bond that may be redeemed by the borrower when interest rates fall, or an interest only mortgage bond that pays no principal at all and has extreme price volatility. The ability to customize cash flows is endless, and because every investor has different needs, Wall Street financial engineers have been able to create products that match borrowers' needs for cash with lenders' very specific interests.

Because of the reliability of the cash flow distribution process, we tend to think of fixed income as "safe", and are always surprised when bonds and fixed income instruments cause the most trouble. We have a good feeling for US Treasury securities but have bad memories of mortgage bonds, collateralized debt obligations, and other instruments that wreaked havoc. It is because their returns and risk are easier to statistically and mathematically model that investors are coaxed into taking more risk than they should. They make bets on reversion to the mean when current valuations look far different from historic relationships. A trade that looks statistically very likely to make money according to investment models somehow loses money as the relationship gaps out to even more statistically unlikely levels. It is always good, especially with fixed income, to understand the investment and strategy.

Though bonds are often discussed as a "risk-free" asset that is not really true, even for credit risk remote issues. Perhaps short-term U.S. Treasury bills can be considered completely safe, but as maturities get longer even "safe" government bonds exhibit more and more interest rate risk, generally referred to as **duration**.

Duration can be considered the weighted average of the time until you receive each of a bond's cash flows, generally referred to in years. For example, the duration of a 10-year zero coupon bond would be 10 years, since there is only one cash flow that occurs 10 years from today. A 10-year bond that made bi-annual payments would have a duration less than 10, because it has intermittent cash flows from interest payments. This brings down the *average* time to receive all the cash flows. The higher the coupon rate, the lower the duration, because each payment between now and maturity pulls the *average* time to maturity of each cash flow closer to the present. For small changes in interest rates the value of a bond (or a bond portfolio) will increase or decrease *approximately* by the following formula:

$$\Delta \text{ Price} = \text{Duration } X \text{ (- } \Delta \text{ Interest Rates)}$$

Larger interest rate changes require an additional calculation known as a convexity adjustment that is beyond the scope of this work. As interest rates increase, a bond price will fall because it's fixed coupon would be less than an investor could find in the market. Why would you buy a bond paying 4% coupon when you can find an equal risk bond offering 5%? The price would decline until the lower coupon bond's yield to maturity would match the new bond, making them roughly equivalent. The more years that you were expecting your fixed coupon to deliver returns (the higher the duration), the larger the price change needed to equate the yield on the old bond versus the new.

A quick example: assume a bond with an 8-year duration, a 4% coupon, and interest rates rise 50 basis points in one day. The bond would fall about 4% in value (8 x .005). Let's now assume interest rates rise 50bp over 3-months. The return of the bond would now be about -3%. Why? Because over three months the bond would have also generated income of 1% (4% annual coupon / 4).[30]

A government bond portfolio with a 5-year duration could fall nearly 5% if interest rates increased 1%. Does a 5 percent decline seem "risk-free"? In truth, if there are no defaults, then a non-callable bond will mature at par, so the loss is temporary. Unless you needed the money now and were forced to sell when prices were low.

Duration is a common concept reported for bond funds. Unfortunately, it only explains the risk in your portfolio due to interest rates. A bond is essentially a loan. Government bonds are loans to a treasury that are supported by the ability to tax, implying that default risk is quite low. Corporate bonds (**credit** is sometimes used as shorthand) on the other hand, are loans to entities that have some default risk. Credit is a compensated risk that exists separately from interest rate risk within fixed income investments. One measure of credit risk sensitivity is called **spread duration.**

Generally, when trading bonds, they are usually priced based on a yield or a spread to a benchmark yield. For example, we often buy government treasury bonds to achieve a certain yield. If we were talking about a newly issued US 10-yr note with a yield of 1% its price may be near par (or 100 cents on the dollar) on its date of issue. However, a 10-yr note issued last month may be priced higher or lower, depending on how interest rates have moved. These two bonds should have yields very similar to each other, so we are concerned much more about the yield than the dollar price. The dollar price is often calculated after the commitment between traders is made on the yield.

---

[30] This example is muddied by both the convexity adjustment, as well as the fact that over time a bond will "roll down the curve". That means that our reference point for valuing bonds changes with time. For example, a 5-year bond would be compared against the 5 year part of the curve. If the coupon was the market rate for a 5 year bond it would be priced at par, but when that bond becomes a 4 year bond after holding for a year, and if the yield curve was upwards sloping, then the coupon may be higher than market for a 4-year bond and trade at a premium because now the coupon was higher than the reference maturity. Over time, the performance of a bond could be affected by duration, convexity, and roll down - *before* taking account the impact of changes in credit spreads - making bond total return analytics challenging.

Similarly, if we were comparing a 10-year corporate bond with a 10-year Treasury, we are concerned with how much more yield we want to earn compared to that "risk-free" Treasury. Let's say we wanted to earn 1%, or 100 basis points *more* in yield than the Treasury. The 100bp is the **spread** we are looking to earn and we would negotiate that number when purchasing the bond. The price would be derived as the trade ticket was created.

While government bonds are subject to interest rate risk, corporate and non-government bonds are subject to the additional spread risk. Spread risk is the value of the bond that is lost when spreads increase, or widen in industry terms. That is, the required return in excess of Treasury bonds has increased. Before we needed 2% in yield (1% from the Treasury and 1% additional for the corporate bond). Now let's say that 100bp spread we agreed to before (over a 10-yr Treasury bond) is now priced at 120bp in the market. The spread has widened 20bp, and we can assume the price of the bond went down because now the required yield is 2.2%. (A spread is said to "widen" if its yield difference compared to its benchmark increases and "tighten" if the difference decreases). Using the same duration formula as before (Δ Price = Duration $* - \Delta$) we know the bond will decrease in value 2%. That may not sound like much, but considering you were only earning 100bp in extra interest each year, you just lost two years of extra income!

Spread risk does not apply to government bonds, by definition. Also, floating rate bonds that have no interest rate risk, can actually have substantial credit risk if the required excess return increases and there is a long maturity. It is hard to eyeball these kinds of exposures and compare one portfolio against another, and for that reason spread duration is an important measure, though rarely reported.

When thinking about risk in a bond fund, understanding the credit risk component is just as important as the interest rate component. It is insufficient to look at duration and be satisfied. Even without knowing all the metrics you'd like to know, some investigation is available. What percent of the portfolio is in corporate bonds? How much extra yield are you earning relative to a comparable maturity Treasury? How much allocation is in lower credit ratings? What does the maturity schedule look like? Choosing the right fixed income investment should be a thoughtful endeavor, not assumed to be automatically safe because it's full of bonds.

If, *over the long term* equities are fairly reliable, why do we use bonds in a portfolio at all? Typically, investors have five reasons to incorporate fixed income in a portfolio, but note that seeking one desired attribute may negate another.

1. **Store of value** – a bond or fixed income investment that has low risk and volatility by design will maintain its value even during market calamity, nor not lose that much. For investors with near term needs or a desire for an emergency fund, these investments hold value. When building a portfolio it may be prudent to have multiple years of living expenses set aside in ultra-short duration bond funds. If an asset liquidation is needed, it is best to sell the investment that is unchanged, instead of one that may be temporarily down 30% (like stocks) or even long term bonds that have fallen 10%.

2. **Stable income** – although selling assets is always an option, an investor may prefer regular disbursements from their accounts to support their lifestyle. Fixed income instruments with steady interest payments play an important role in delivering this goal. There are important caveats to this: steady income can be eroded in value because of inflation, and higher risk, higher yielding fixed income investments can reduce or eliminate their payments if the issuer is under financial or economic stress.

3. **Negative correlation to stocks** – as discussed earlier, assets that have a negative correlation to the market offer a significant reduction in volatility. Often, long duration US Treasury bonds go up in price as stock market volatility increases. Portfolios with some of this exposure can have a higher Sharpe Ratio. Historically, portfolio strategists have suggested a 60% equity / 40% bond portfolio as a powerful allocation and you often see this suggested to many clients. In the past with higher interest rates (some decades higher than 10%), even years when interest rates climbed the income generated compensated for the price impact. The steady march lower in rates has created continuous price gains nearly every year, giving bonds good performance even with rates low. Paired with volatile equities the steady, countercyclical nature of bonds improved the risk/return characteristics of the portfolio. As of 2022 however, with interest rates substantially lower than historic experience

and inflation higher, the ability of a long duration bond to continue to go up in value is limited, and the income generated is minimal.

4. **Reduce portfolio volatility** – an investor may have the horizon to maintain a large weight to stocks, but just might not have the stomach for it. An individual with a $1,000,000 portfolio may simply not be able to mentally ride out a $300,000 decline. If seeing that loss on his statement would force him to sell his positions, only to miss the rebound, then a higher allocation to bonds would protect him from his impulses.

5. **Excess returns** – many fixed income products can generate high yields or even returns in excess of their coupon payments. For example, taking credit risk will offer higher interest payments, but also offers further upside when credit conditions improve and the yield spread declines. This can enhance portfolio returns, but should be taken judiciously. Chasing yield has many unintended consequences, and can negate all four of the benefits above. All else being equal, if a bond has higher yield, it most likely has a higher correlation to equities. It is more likely to lose value in an economic downturn. Moreover, It will not reduce portfolio volatility as much as expected because it is most correlated with the stock market when markets are at their weakest. Investing in junk bonds or leveraged products that push yields higher substantially increase portfolio risk, but the danger is you still think you have relatively safe bonds. These risky products truly need supervision. Each product is different but investors must think about the risks – fixed income products should not get a pass on due diligence.

By far the most important use of fixed income is to maintain a liquid, *accessible* store of value. That is why it is very curious to see fixed income surrogates embedded in illiquid vehicles. Consider, for example, variable annuities. With surrender charges making short-term access to your principal prohibitive you are forced to keep a long horizon view of those funds. But some of these products offer fixed income options. In this case, there is no liquidity, there is no immediate steady income, and fees erode much of the fixed income return – violating most of the reasons to hold fixed income.

Another common occurrence is the inclusion of fixed income investments in a tax deferred account, such as a 401k or Traditional IRA **for young individuals.** [31] Withdrawing funds from these accounts before age 59 ½ incurs penalties, so there is limited accessibility of the assets. If the goal is to minimize the dollar value of the volatility of the portfolio (Invest in bonds to ensure your portfolio is unlikely to lose more than $30,000 for example), then why keep adding to stocks each year? If the intention is to reduce percentage volatility (Invest in bonds to ensure the portfolio is unlikely to lose more than 30% for example) a 25 year old is giving up decades of higher return compounding to stabilize money he won't touch for 40 years.

We should also be wary of terms like "fixed income surrogate" that go far afield from traditional fixed income exposure. With interest rates so low some investors use assets like stocks from Utility companies or Real Estate Investment Trusts to replace the income. While this may serve one aspect of an investor's need for fixed (steady) income, it may violate the others. Both may be considered lower volatility, or somewhat uncorrelated to the rest of the market, and yet both can see high betas and 20-30% drawdowns.

While the ultimate goal of equities is always clear (higher returns), fixed income has a hybrid existence. It serves multiple purposes, some oppositional to each other. Though the rewards may be smaller, the thought that must go into them should be higher because they are often complex, and in idiosyncratic ways.

---

[31] Placing equities in tax deferred accounts like Traditional IRAs will recast favorable capital gains returns as less tax favorable ordinary income, implying a preference for fixed income investments in those accounts. If an investor is expected to be in a low tax bracket at retirement, the decision has less impact. Clients expected to maintain high income after retirement will have a different analysis. The choice of asset location is different for each client and is an important part of financial planning.

Many advisors choose to invest fixed income assets in actual individual bonds, which has advantages but many disadvantages. The upside is direct control over the timing of maturities and risk. Individual bonds have an advantage in yield and issue selection, and given the single maturity of each bond the return and principal are more reliably estimated. But it poses on-going maintenance and surveillance issues, lacks diversification, and could pose liquidity problems. Individual bonds may not have a robust market and to execute a trade a broker may have to find a buyer willing to purchase the security, and the price offered may not be reflective of value. To work around these problems some advisors use funds, either mutual funds or ETFs, to invest the fixed income allocation.

Traditional fixed income fund investing (either ETFs or mutual funds) may be broken down into general categories, based on interest rate sensitivity or product specificity. The following six descriptions could describe the investment focus of most funds available, but is by no means comprehensive.

Money Market funds are invested with very strict criteria so there is very little chance of "breaking the buck" – that is they are designed so that the net asset value per share is kept to $1.00 and any excess from interest income or price gains is distributed. Losses create a perilous situation for money market funds which are typically considered nearly risk free. However, those limitations prevent the funds from investing in not-so-risk-free but completely reasonable products.

"Ultra Short" funds are often substituted for money market funds. Ultra-Short funds provide a bit more return but can have a slight amount of volatility. Though minimal in general, Ultra-Short funds still fell 3-4% at the beginning of the COVID-19 pandemic in March 2020. The recovery was quick, but some investors relying on those funds to act like cash were very concerned.

Short Duration funds make no promises of being a cash substitute. They typically have durations of 2-3 years, so maintain some interest rate risk but with the benefit of higher yielding investment options. Given that the portfolio assets have a longer term to maturity, they also have higher spread duration. While Ultra-Short funds were down 3-4% during the Covid volatility, Short Duration funds were down twice as much – about 8-10%. Given that interest rates were falling at the time (indicating that prices *should* have been rising) this weakness was due to spread widening – investors demanded extra compensation to buy risky securities.

Laddered Maturity ETFs are somewhat new. Rather than holding a portfolio of bonds with maturities ranging from one to twenty years, ETF sponsors such as Blackrock and Invesco create funds where every bond in the fund is a sampling of index constituents that matures within a given year. At the end of the maturity year the entire ETF is liquidated and returned to investors. Investors could create a ladder out through ten years, or choose specific years where the yield appears more attractive, or keep a short three to five year ladder as a low duration fixed income allocation. These structures allow customization, control, and diversification for financial advisors to tailor portfolios for specific client cash flow needs. The investor still has interest rate risk and loss of value can occur, but as the ETF approaches its set maturity date the price would pull back towards its "par" value.

Core funds are the very familiar package of government, corporate, and mortgage bonds benchmarked against indexes like the old Lehman Aggregate Bond Index ("the Lehman Agg" for short, now the unwieldy Bloomberg Barclays Aggregate Bond Index). The benchmark includes all the large bond issues originated and still active. The composition of the index drifts each month as new issues slowly change the average composition. As corporate issuers lock in lower interest rates on their corporate debt with longer maturity new bond offerings, you see the index slowly increase in duration. As energy companies become junk rated issuers, they fall out of the index. These bond indexes reflect the changes we see in global debt origination. Many of these core funds will tend to look much like these indexes, though some will make aggressive deviations from benchmark based on their research and market views. These funds have been around for decades and have served clients very well, especially as interest rates have done nothing but fall. However, they don't all have the same risks, and may not fit a client's needs. The duration of these funds can be much longer than is appropriate, introducing interest rate risk that is not sufficiently compensated, or does not correspond to the client's liquidity needs or withdrawal rate.

(Most) **Municipals bonds** offer tax free income, even within a mutual fund or ETF. It is almost always free of federal tax and free of state tax if the bond is within your state of residence [32] .   For this reason municipal bond yields look unappealingly low at first glance. Some high income investors may gravitate to the product, but the advisor should do the calculation to verify they are actually offering better return for investors. Dividing the stated yield on the bond by (1 – tax rate) will help you compare a muni yield with a similar rated corporate bond. For example, a muni yield of 2% with a marginal tax rate of 40% would have a tax equivalent yield of 3.30%. If the marginal tax rate was 30% instead, the tax equivalent yield would only be 2.86%. These differences do matter. If a client is in California the benefits of a California municipal bond can be tremendous due to the combined federal and state tax rate even though the nominal rate has been driven very low. That same bond may be a huge mistake for anyone else out of state.

Of note, **Preferred Stock** can sometimes be used as a surrogate for fixed income securities. There are different risks at play here – preferred stock is lowest in seniority compared to other fixed income investments and some do not have a guarantee of payment. The yields are often higher, but so is the volatility. It is also a smaller, less liquid market with sizable bid/ask spreads. Preferred Stock is generally considered to be in the middle of the capital structure: higher priority than common equities, but lower priority than bondholders. Like any other investment, be mindful of client needs and tolerances.

---

[32] There are exceptions so bond investors should be careful to ensure each individual bond is indeed tax free.

A SIDE NOTE ON FIXED INCOME

When advising on a client's wealth we should incorporate all aspects of their financial position. Even if you were only managing taxable assets, you can't ignore the existence of 401ks and other assets managed or held away from you. Ideally you would include those elements as part of the portfolio that you construct for them so the client's total wealth is managed harmoniously.

Another factor to account for is our clients' debt – mortgages, car payments, collateralized borrowing, etc. When we buy bonds and other fixed income products, we are essentially lending money. Therefore, debt is the opposite of a fixed income investment and can be considered alongside the portfolio, to the extent it negates some of our investment efforts.

To review quickly, we own fixed income for a **store of value, steady income, negative correlation to stocks, to reduce portfolio volatility, or to generate total returns.** To some extent, we can accomplish these by paying off existing debts.

For example, if a five-year car loan carried an interest of 4% per year, but we owned a bond mutual fund yielding 2%, what would happen if we sold the mutual fund to pay off the debt? We would:

a. Lose store of value because the mutual fund is easier to liquidate than getting a new loan
b. Increase income because the interest rate on the loan is higher than the yield on the fund
c. Lose the negative correlation to stocks
d. Improved portfolio stability because you have eliminated the volatility of the mutual fund and locked in a risk-free 4% return
e. Raised income but lost the opportunity to generate price returns

Each client is different but some may view the returns from investing in their own debt is more valuable than the mutual fund. Others may rather not give up the liquidity. Knowing your clients' priorities will help guide you, or simply talking about these decisions may be fruitful.

A larger question seems to generate emphatic responses from advisors – should clients pay off their mortgage, or should they send extra principal with each payment? Here the question is not comparing one debt for another because we are not necessarily suggesting this needs to be paid for against a fixed income allocation. Instead we are comparing carrying personal debt vs the opportunity cost of uninvested cash, in the case where the client has the excess means to pay off principal where it would not affect their desired lifestyle.

Let us say there was 20 years left on the mortgage at an interest rate of 3%[33]. Paying it off would essentially generate income (because you would no longer make monthly payments) but you would lose liquidity (as the cash used to pay off the loan is no longer available unless you took out a new loan) and you would lose the option of investing at higher returns. Over 20 years, it is very likely that an investment in the stock market would outperform the 3% interest rate on the mortgage. Paying off a mortgage early must be viewed in that context – a guaranteed return that aids cash flow, or alternatively investing at a higher rate with higher risk but maintaining easy access to the principal. Net worth would most likely be maximized by not paying off the mortgage and investing at the higher return, if given a long horizon.

The decision changes as the mortgage gets closer to being paid off. Let's say there were only 5 years left. One can no longer say with confidence that the equity market would most likely outperform, as volatility of returns over any five-year period can be high. In that case it could make sense to pay it off with cash or by selling a fixed income asset in the portfolio. Using equities would entail a higher cost in terms of potential returns – and should be considered against the financial plan assumptions.

Another way to think about this is a discussion of leverage. When we use debt to buy things like cars and homes we are controlling more assets for the same dollar value of net worth. The leverage amplifies gains and losses as a percent of your net worth – instead of selling stock to buy a home or pay off a mortgage, you are maintaining debt on your personal balance sheet and simultaneously keep the stock or other assets and its performance. As long as the cost of the debt is less than the gain on the portfolio, leverage helps add to net worth. When one has

---

[33] It should be noted that since mortgage payments include principal, the *average* life of a mortgage would be about half of the total years left

the financial resources to pay off a debt, one asset (let's say stocks from your portfolio) decreases, but net worth stays the same because debt declined as well. Even if we used cash to pay off the mortgage, we had the option of investing in stocks, but chose not to, foregoing that potentially higher return.

From this perspective the improved cash flow from paying off the debt is incidental because higher equity values can be monetized (sold in the market at will) to make debt payments. The danger, of course, is if the market falls or the assets become impaired, and the client is no longer able to service the debt. When we reduce leverage through paying off a mortgage, our goal may be to reduce net worth volatility, or we believe that the potential for gains is lower than the cost of debt over the time horizon used.

Often the choice to pay off the mortgage is couched in terms of financial stability – being able to retire debt free is a wonderful thing. Reducing debt has the statistical effect of shifting the likely growth of your net worth lower, but reducing the probability of very bad scenarios and very good scenarios – a narrower distribution of outcomes. Clearly, some clients would benefit from more certainty while others have the means to be more aggressive. Blanket statements about best and worst financial tactics are not helpful.

These decisions are available if the client's choice is between paying down debt or investing for higher return. If the choice is between paying down debt or immediate personal spending, it is no longer a risk preference decision, but a spending timing decision. I include this section to encourage advisors to think holistically about a client's financial position. The tradeoffs within a portfolio are very similar to other financial decisions faced. We should be aware if portfolio investments can or should be better allocated to maximize wealth.

Inflation investing is an odd addition to this discussion, but when seeking to build diversified portfolios it is a relevant concern. We should be thinking about not just zigs and zags in asset prices, but also various macroeconomic conditions. When economic growth is robust, stocks are strong. Stocks can still do well with mild inflation as companies pass on higher costs to consumers. When interest rates are falling (and the economy is weak), fixed income does well. But what happens when the price level is rising dramatically?

Fixed income is clearly vulnerable to high inflation scenarios. Equities may be protected from mild inflation, but they are still at risk in high inflation environments. For this reason, though probably not explicitly explained, financial advisors and portfolio managers sometimes suggest various inflation hedging assets to incorporate in the mix.

We will discuss briefly three asset classes which have been considered effective hedges against inflation: Treasury Inflation Protected Securities (TIPS), Real Estate, and Commodities

Treasury Inflation-Protected Securities

The most direct method of gaining inflation protection is by allocating capital to bonds that adjust their value based on changes in inflation measures. The United States Treasury issues Treasury Inflation-Protected Securities, or TIPS. These bonds often have very low coupons (a measure of the **real interest rate**)[34] and adjust the principal higher based on growth in the Consumer Price Index (CPI)[35].

---

[34] Quoted interest rates are usually "nominal" interest rates, in that they include an inflation assumption. A lender may receive a nominal rate of interest, but over time that return is eroded by the effects of inflation. If the lender received 3% interest but inflation was 2%, he has only earned about 1% in terms of purchasing power. The "real" rate strips out the inflation from the nominal rate, providing a more useful indication of return for a lender, or cost of funds for a borrower.

[35] The US Bureau of Labor Statistics publishes the CPI monthly. It is a survey of prices for a basket of goods and services representing each sector of the economy. Changes in the index reflect observed inflation affecting consumers.

The face value of these securities increase at the same rate as CPI, providing an inflation hedge to the rest of the portfolio.

These securities also offer market information about expected inflation. Subtracting the yield of a TIP from the yield of a nominal Treasury bond results in a "breakeven rate of inflation". If actual inflation is higher than the breakeven rate, then TIPS will outperform regular treasury bonds. If inflation is lower than the breakeven rate, TIPS will underperform. Theoretically, the collective wisdom and trading activity of investors would push the breakeven rate to a level where the market forecasts inflation will be. An investor in TIPS would either believe inflation will be higher than the breakeven suggests, or simply be using it as an inflation hedge, just in case.

An unusual characteristic of TIPS is their reported yield can be negative. To be clear, the investor is not experiencing a negative return. It would occur any time the nominal yield is lower than the expected inflation rate. For example, if the 5-year Treasury had a yield of 1% and inflation over the next five years was expected to be 1.5%, the yield on the TIP would be about -0.5%, but that is a real yield. The investor would be compensated by the inflation adjustment to the principal, as discussed.

It is very unlikely that an investment in TIPS would generate a negative return if held to maturity, but the return can still be lower than the inflation rate if real rates are negative. TIPS can also experience volatility in pricing caused by changes in the market real yield for that maturity. Also note that *deflation* can reduce the face value of a TIP, though it can never fall below par. Investors buying seasoned bonds that have accrued a significant amount of inflation principal would need to be aware of that risk.

Real Estate

Real Estate is also a common inflation hedge. Some real estate investments such as REITs (real estate investment trusts) can be considered a fixed income surrogate because they may provide steady income, and real estate can become more valuable when interest rates fall, giving it duration like bonds. However, often when the economy is doing poorly, real estate can be vulnerable and weaken in price, just like equities, limiting its diversification qualities. However, one of the components of inflation is the rental cost of housing and shelter. One of the benefits of owning real estate is the steady receipt of rent, which should increase as inflation goes higher. Under moderate inflation scenarios, the improving cash flows from real estate can provide relief for an investor as other assets fall in value.

Although not always considered an investment asset, our primary residence is still a real estate asset. We may not notice its inflation fighting attributes, but if a client was renting a home he would surely notice his annual increase in rent. Homeowners are protected from those price shocks as their mortgages are typically locked in at fixed rates[36]. When developing a financial plan, anticipating inflation would be much more significant for those who had not locked down their housing costs.

Like equities, real estate offers returns generated from profits (rent instead of dividends) plus the appreciation of the asset. Since private market real estate is not priced continually like public markets, an investment made through private channels (either directly owning, through partnerships, or non-traded REITs) can generate solid returns in most environments with less volatility than stocks. This can help stabilize a portfolio's value without giving up as much return as bonds. But investors should be aware that lower appraisals and valuation adjustments may not occur immediately in a weak market but will eventually be reflected in the net asset value. Investing in publicly traded REITs may offer a similar exposure, but with a potentially accelerated and exaggerated response to the market environment.

Commodities

Commodities (generally food, energy, and metals) and especially gold, are often used as inflation hedges. Gold is especially considered a store of value. When inflation heats up, the value of the dollar declines, requiring more dollars to purchase stable value assets like gold. Commodities prices also reflect higher inflation, almost by definition. As the units of currency required to buy assets increase, it makes sense that owning *things* that could cost more money helps protect a portfolio. However, commodities are subject to supply dynamics – if it suddenly becomes easier to provide those commodities, or there are more

---

[36] Those with adjustable rate mortgages are not as protected, and must carefully consider if early year low rates were enough compensation for a future rate shock.

people providing them, commodity prices can go through long and difficult periods of weakness. For example, investors in oil may have been confident in their trade believing a healthy economy would increase demand, but innovations in US fracking technology and alternative fuels rapidly increased supply of energy, creating a volatile path for investors. But as inflation took hold in 2021 and 2022 using oil and commodities as a hedge would have eventually provided some protection.

As mentioned, the return of Commodities is determined by the supply and demand for those materials. But owning the commodity provides no actual income – it only has a return when it is sold. But there are implied costs to owning commodities. If you were investing in livestock there would be feed and transportation costs. Owning bulk commodities would have warehousing costs. In addition, the capital outlay would include an implied cost of funds – you cannot make an investment without giving up the opportunity to invest in something else.

When we invest in commodities we are not expecting to actually take delivery of a warehouse full of product and hold it indefinitely. It is typically accessed through funds that invest in the forward and futures market – financial derivatives that allow for settlement sometime in the future. Delivery contract pricing will embed the cost of holding that commodity until the contract expires, including the implied cost of funding that strategy. Therefore while the other inflation hedging strategies may offer a positive return regardless of the inflation rate, many commodities have a headwind that requires a moderate level of inflation to just break even.

Beta to Inflation

We have discussed Beta as a portfolio's response to the overall market, but beta more generically is a statistical measure of the relationship between a dependent variable and an independent variable in a regression. This concept is very useful in hedging portfolios against risk, and we can also use it to evaluate and scale exposure to an inflation hedge.

If we examine the returns of different asset classes (the dependent variable) against the inflation rate experienced during that time period (the independent variable) we can see how responsive that asset is to changes in inflation. The implication is that assets that have a higher response to changes in the inflation rate are more effective at providing a portfolio with inflation protection, *and we need less of it to effectively hedge!*

Invesco has published wonderful research on the betas to inflation of the typical suite of inflation hedges.[37] Using annual data from 1998 through 2021 they analyzed the returns of standard asset indexes against the annual change in the CPI. TIPS had the lowest positive return, rising just 1.58% for a 1% rise in the price level. Gold surprisingly had a lower response than equities, 2.88% vs 2.91%. Real estate was more effective at 5.79%. But commodities were much more reactive, 8.97% for the Bloomberg Commodity Index (BCOM). On the other end of the spectrum, bonds had a negative response to inflation (as expected) of -.37%.

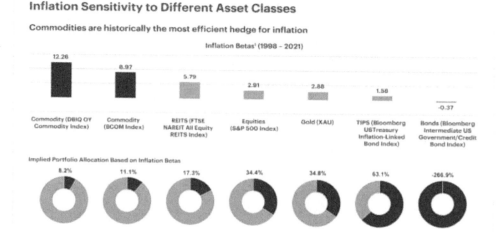

Inflation Sensitivity to Different Asset Classes

Commodities are historically the most efficient hedge for inflation

The more important takeaway from this is the implied portfolio allocation you need to incorporate to hedge inflation. If you intended to use TIPS for your inflation protection with a beta of 1.58%, 63% of your portfolio would need to be invested to ensure your portfolio was adequately hedged.[38] So while TIPS offer protection, the impact is rather marginal. However, a 23% allocation to TIPS as

---

[37] Commodities Corner: The Race Continues (Key Themes for 2022) - March 25, 2022
https://www.invesco.com/us/en/insights/commodities-corner-the-race-continues.html
[38] If target hedge is 100% of the portfolio and TIPS offers more than 1 for 1 protection,
100% / 1.58% = ~63%

part of your bond portfolio would offset the inflation sensitivity of your bond allocation (-.37 / 1.58)[39].

Using these betas, we see that equities only require a 34% allocation, real estate a 17% allocation, and commodities only need an 11% allocation, to protect from inflation's predations. These betas are not absolute, and subject to the time period tested and the proxy measures used. In addition, data sometimes just doesn't behave. But these numbers can give us a sense of scale of impact. An advisor may wonder, how much should he invest in commodities? Knowing that he already has exposures to stocks and real estate, he can gauge how much protection he has, how much more he may want, and how much he should allocate to achieve a desired posture.

The ability to hedge inflation is a useful arrow in an investor's quiver. Successfully managing that risk can stabilize a portfolio over the long term, especially during periods of extreme price level movements. However, some periods in history would have made the choice difficult given the strong (though volatile) performance from both stocks and bonds.

---

[39] Using statistics to hedge an exposure is useful, but only as effective as the power of the regression to explain the relationship. Some hedge ratios derived this way may be unstable, and hence unreliable, leading to an over or underhedged position – either of which could lead to unexpected losses. Investors should be very careful defining and modeling relationships to ensure confidence in a hedge before placing trades. Hedge ratios are more often used in a trading environment, but conceptually useful for portfolio managers to be aware of.

Up to now we have been discussing investing with risks and specific instruments in mind. Straightforward asset classes like stocks and bonds are easily understood and categorized, even if their risk is not as simple as advertised. As financial market sophistication has increased and access to non-traditional assets has become more widespread, some investors have jumped aggressively into "Alternative Investments". The purpose of Alternatives is to either reach sources of return that are typically unavailable, or make investments that are uncorrelated to public markets, reducing volatility without sacrificing return.

Not everyone can invest in Alternative Investments. The hurdle for entry is often based on net worth estimates. Two common categories are Accredited Investor (requiring a net worth over $1 million or two years having earned over $300,000 for a married couple) and Qualified Purchaser (a client has $5 million in investment assets). The purpose of these constraints is to protect investors, but also limit regulatory hurdles for the partnerships and funds that create these vehicles. Given the complexity and lack of liquidity inherent in such vehicles, restricting Alternatives to certain types of investors is certainly appropriate.

Typically, when we discuss alternatives we are often talking about Private Equity and Hedge Funds. But alternatives could also include direct investments in private companies, real estate and real estate investment trusts, commodities including timber, and Master Limited Partnerships (MLPs) that invest in oil and gas infrastructure. Any asset that can generate income or returns that has low correlation to public markets can be included in the list. Even precious metals, patents and intellectual property, and collectibles like artwork, rare coins, and antiques can be included.

Years ago, alternatives had been offered strictly to the ultra-wealthy and institutions but they have lately been marketed to a wider base. The largest wealth management companies have partnered with alternative investment managers to provide access to these instruments. The wealth managers provide a client base that is looking to diversify their portfolios, making it easier for alternative managers to market funds to new investors without having to develop and educate the investors themselves.

Alternatives asset managers have also engaged a wider audience by embedding their strategies within mutual funds. These funds, commonly called Liquid Alts, provide access and liquidity to investors who wish to participate in the same kind of uncorrelated or lower correlated alpha strategies. These are often hedge fund type trading strategies rather than long term non-public investments. There are also publicly traded closed end funds called Business Development Companies (BDCs) that do invest in more speculative debt and non-traded equity instruments, akin to private equity offerings. These funds can have high distribution yields but also substantial risk.

For non-traded alternatives some marketing trumpets the benefits of its low correlation to public markets, but these proclamations should be taken with a grain of salt. If an asset is priced only irregularly, then mathematically sure, it will have low correlation. This alone does not make such an investment an appropriate addition to the portfolio. One must think conceptually in these cases. What is the investment strategy, and does it make sense for it to be uncorrelated? How often and when are the underlying assets priced? Does the strategy state a beta target? What percentage of the portfolio should be allocated to non-correlated assets?

One problem with good strategies is they seem well thought out and successful with robust risk management, but managers often try to generate higher returns through leverage, by borrowing funds to reinvest in the strategy with the expectations that returns would more than compensate for the cost of funds. When surprises occur portfolio managers will have to liquidate their assets at very low prices, eroding the investors' equity. With alternative investments, investment managers have been given a tremendous amount of freedom to invest as they see fit with little transparency. One important question is not how much risk your clients can bear, but how much volatility can the investment structure absorb before it cracks. A client may say "I can handle risk!" but ironically, the investment might not.

Alternatives may have a place in a portfolio, but more than any other asset class blind faith in the marketing can lead to perilous outcomes. The following chapters are necessarily brief summaries of these instruments and not meant to fully elaborate their nuances and risks.

Generally, private equity is funding for investments in non-public entities. It could be venture capital, used to fund nascent start-ups that need capital and advice to grow out its business plan. It could be "buy-out" capital that is used to carve out pieces of existing businesses to be a stand-alone entity or reconfigured with other business units to achieve economies of scale. It could be "middle-markets" investing in companies that have been around but have never been able to break out. There are plenty of strategies that all fall under the rubric of private equity, but they do have common features in structure and process. Often private equity sponsors have a strategic vision or a depth of experience that can transform neglected assets into entities that are more profitable if strategically placed. For example, Blackstone acquired the benefits management arm of Aon, where it had no visibility within the company, and rebranded it as Alight Solutions and allowed it to thrive with an effective, incentivized business strategy.

Private equity investors (called "limited partners" because they make no management decisions) do not submit their investment payment all at once, but instead make a commitment that is periodically "called" by the "general partner" (the private equity sponsor that manages the investment) when a target is identified and funds are needed. It may take five years for all the capital to be called, and another five to seven years for the investment to be returned with profits. During this time the principal is completely unavailable to the investor. An investor must be able to live without access to his investment for a decade before committing. There is a secondary market, but it is very inefficient and sellers need to accept low prices to get out from the capital commitments and have their principal returned.

The staggered and unpredictable schedule of calls and distributions also makes it hard to judge performance. At what point do you start counting returns, if there were multiple times when investments were made, and returns on investment are distributed periodically (but irregularly) over a decade? The industry has settled on using a metric called Internal Rate of Return (IRR), which reflects how long every dollar was invested and how fast those funds were returned. Unfortunately, the IRR is subject to nuance that makes return numbers not always comparable to a calculation on a fully invested investment account.

Many times advocates of private equity emphasize that it is uncorrelated to the equity markets. This is at best an exaggeration. In down markets investors may note that their private equity positions have not moved lower in price, but that merely reflects the fact that they are not priced daily. Or monthly. Sometimes not quarterly. A target company investment in a private equity fund may not be appraised more than once a year. Not moving in price does not mean the eventual realized returns are not correlated to the market. Eventually, private equity investors are compensated when the underlying investments in the fund are liquidated, usually through an initial public offering in a healthy market. Market values of portfolio companies are also imputed from valuations of similar companies traded on an exchange. If the market is very expensive during the acquisition stage, the private equity firm may end up paying too much, and lose money if the market is weak when they look for a liquidity event.

For this reason, private equity investors should understand the costs of the product – liquidity is nearly non-existent, tracking the performance is delayed and difficult to interpret, and the result will be at least somewhat correlated.

To put private equity in context of what we've discussed, private equity allows you to benefit from both systematic and idiosyncratic risk. In public markets firm specific risk is diversified away, but that's not possible in private equity. When a private equity fund manager is looking for investments, they are cognizant of the risks and opportunities of that specific company. As they underwrite the purchase they will use (ostensibly) conservative estimates of cost savings potential and revenue growth as well as a discount rate that is appropriate for that company's actual risk. By allowing an investor to earn both systematic and unsystematic returns, private equity thus unlocks performance that stock market indexes can't offer.

Historically private equity has indeed outperformed public markets, though some academic research indicates the returns are similar to small-cap equities after adjusting for leverage. Cambridge Analytics publishes detailed reports on which PE strategies have outperformed and provide good context. One caveat is the divergence between returns reported by the private equity sponsor from that received by a high net worth investor who pays additional access fees and up front commissions to their brokerage for the ability to participate.

Another reminder is that private equity funds can be focused on specific sectors. Suddenly the risk is not a market risk, or based on the sponsor's ability to execute, but the macro factors of the investment strategy. Energy funds will be affected by the price and demand of oil and gas, for example. Real Estate funds will be sensitive to factors like interest rates and demographics. As with any decision about investment inclusion, it is not the wrapper but what's inside that determines your risk.

Before the Great Financial Crisis, the banking system provided or facilitated much of the debt financing needs of smaller and middle-market companies. Banks either provided loans directly or underwrote them in large syndicated loan deals. Following the crisis, banks found themselves restrained from participating either because of the Volcker rule which restricted banks from engaging in riskier activity, or constrained by the Basel III banking regulations which made some lending services onerous and costly to offer.

At the same time, private equity's engagement with the broader economy has become more common. The various strategies employed by private equity often require a large sum of debt financing to facilitate, at the same time bank financing has become less available. Syndicated lending remains an avenue as well as high yield bond offerings.[40] But much of the need for capital from smaller private companies has been provided by "private credit".

Private credit is a catch-all term for non-securitized debt investments made in non-public entities outside the banking system. This could include:

- Direct Lending – loans made to companies that are generally senior secured
- Mezzanine Debt – loans made that are subordinate to other debt obligation in the capital structure
- Distressed Debt – investments in debt instruments of financially troubled companies that are purchased at discount
- Real Estate – debt used to finance real estate development, acquisition, or refinancing
- Esoteric asset-backed – debt used to finance the purchase of specific assets that generate reliable cash flows, and are collateralized by that asset

---

[40] Investors could participate in the loan market by buying ETFs or mutual funds that specialize in this part of the market, often labeled "senior loan" or "bank loan" funds. They could also invest with CLOs or Collateralized Loan Obligations, which tranche up syndicated loans packages, creating different levels of risk.

Typically private credit investors are concentrating on the Direct Lending component. Direct lending is differentiated by the fact the investment manager has an on-going relationship with the borrower and has not been presented the idea by an intermediary or relying on other entities to perform the due diligence or ongoing surveillance. This gives the Direct Lendor more intelligence about their investment decision and more involvement in management of the risks.

Investors in private credit are attracted to the Floating Rate nature of many of these loans, which reduces interest rate risk as the monthly rate resets eliminate duration exposure. The bilateral nature of the negotiations protects the investors and can lead to better covenants, and the lack of competing interests (as there are few if any other lenders participating in the loan) add clarity for the investor in case of default. Finally, these loans are typically made with coupon payments 600-700bp over the benchmark rate, offering a generous return for investors regardless of interest rate environment. There are often origination fees and prepayment penalties that further enhance the return.

For borrowers, the attributes of private credit also provide benefits. Once a lender is engaged, the time to execution can be very quick. This contrasts with execution through the banking system, where bankers typically have layers of approval that must be navigated. Broadly syndicated or underwritten deals may be dependent on market conditions and time consuming roadshows. Also, the bilateral nature allows more flexibility to the borrower, as there is only one counterparty to negotiate with.

Investing in Private Credit is often through BDC's mentioned previously, or through Interval Funds, that look like mutual funds having tickers and can be purchased (but not sold) daily. BDCs will often require client signatures (when not publicly traded), can have more leverage, and are generally more focused in their investment choices. Interval funds have more discretion on how funds are deployed. Most private credit funds will have liquidity (the ability to sell your position) only quarterly, to accommodate the lack of secondary markets for the underlying portfolio loans.

The attractive features of private credit for both lender and borrower has allowed it to become a more common resource for CFOs, and more common in investors' portfolios. The absence of banks' participation accompanied by the desperate need from borrowers has created a ballooning in the number of Private Credit funds in the market. Existing institutional money managers are building dedicated private credit teams. Wealth managers have realized this opportunity and elevated it from a niche part of the fixed income tool-kit.

Hedge funds have been around for decades, but developed a mystique and a notoriety perhaps in the 1990s. On one hand you think of hedge fund billionaires trading aggressively, either on the phone or on their yacht. On the other hand you remember hedge fund failures like Long Term Capital Management that seemed to blow up the entire financial system with a few highly levered trades.[41]

The term invokes images of swashbuckling traders generating tremendous returns and charging tremendous fees (typically 2% of assets and 20% of performance, but that is coming down). The truth is more mundane. There are about 3,600 hedge funds in the United States, compared to about 7,900 mutual funds. Hedge funds exist to do things mutual funds can't, such as use leverage to increase returns, derivatives to allow more flexibility in investment, and sell companies short to create hedged market neutral trades. The hedge fund investment vehicle is also notable for requiring less disclosure and limiting the frequency of investors' redemptions, and requiring significant minimum investment size.

Investments traded on an exchange can be made available any trading day of the week. In contrast, hedge funds may limit the liquidity window to quarterly redemptions, impose a years long lock-up or impose substantial early redemption fees, causing investors to wait months to receive their proceeds. Switching can entail costs – meaningful upfront commissions could be charged again on a new fund, plus the investor will be out of the market during the transition. This lack of liquidity is a function of the types of investments hedge funds pursue. Some of the underlying investments are illiquid themselves, some are sensitive trading positions that cannot be easily unwound. The certainty of being able to maintain

---

[41] Long Term Capital Management (LTCM), whose partners included Nobel Prize winning economists, was a successful hedge fund in the late 1990s, amassing $4.7 Billion in equity but controlled $129 billion in assets through leverage. In 1998 the fund failed as a result of the Russian bond crisis in that year. The resulting market dislocation forced the Federal Reserve to coordinate an unwinding with Wall Street banks to prevent a more widespread event.

positions allows the hedge fund to approach investment without having to worry that investors could demand cash at any moment.

There are many types of hedge funds (and this is not an exhaustive list):

- **Long/Short**: taking long and short positions, hoping to have a steadier return
- **Market-neutral funds**: that seek to have a net zero beta
- **Event-driven strategies:** profit from specific circumstances
- **Credit-driven**: debt investments subject to default risk
- **Fixed Income relative value:** make highly-levered bets on small movements in relative valuation of fixed income instruments that deviate from historical averages
- **Global Macro:** uses all markets to make geographic and political bets
- **Quantitative**: uses computer models to identify asset mispricing utilizing thousands of simultaneous trades
- **Fund of Funds and Multi-strategy**: funds specialized in choosing other hedge funds to invest in, or where a single firm develops a portfolio of strategies to be offered in a single investment vehicle

Investors should be aware of the *kind* of beta that is maintained in the strategy – be it equity, corporate credit, interest rates – as it will invariably overlap with other investments in their portfolio.

Investors will typically use hedge funds for two reasons – 1. they are aiming for outsized returns, 2. They are seeking to maximize their Sharpe Ratio with uncorrelated returns.

Some funds seek to generate truly out-sized results. These funds are easier to understand as there are fewer conceptual structures to wade through. They can have tremendous volatility and they either outperform equities over a relevant lookback period, or they have failed that. Even when they've succeeded, an investor should know why they succeeded. I once reviewed an asset-backed security (ABS) hedge fund that advertised 17% annualized returns. On inspection, its inception was the year following the financial crisis in which it had phenomenal gains, that would never be duplicated. Success is more suspicious than failure. That same fund saw disastrous results during the COVID-19 swoon that it has not yet recovered from.

Other investors use hedge funds to generate a high Sharpe Ratio, either through owning an uncorrelated asset that improves their total portfolio's volatility, or simply looking for an efficient add-on investment. These funds truly try to be "hedge" funds, that look to reduce volatility and achieve solid, uncorrelated results. These funds usually have a lower beta, and try to generate returns through mostly Alpha, that is—returns that can be generated regardless of market direction. Long/short equity funds generically function this way. Regardless of the investment universe (health care, emerging markets quantitative arbitrage, etc) the goal is to maintain a target beta, usually lower than the market, and outperform with security selection. *Risk premia* is a term for investment strategies that use exploitable historic relationships created by persistent behaviors or structural conditions of the market. These returns are expected to be independent of actual market moves. Unfortunately many of these low beta strategies still have experienced correlation in down markets and have struggled to keep up with equities in up markets lately.

A subtle distinction exists between mathematical beta and correlation. Beta measures how *much* an investment moves with the market, correlation measures how *often* they move together. Low beta strategies can present themselves as a fixed income surrogate, offering 3% over cash yields with low volatility. These strategies can be suspect, as they may be uncorrelated to other markets during normal times, but exceptionally correlated during times of duress. For example, there are many "liquid alt" funds, mutual funds that invest in multiple hedge funds with various (ideally uncorrelated) strategies. Over the last five years many have had steady results somewhat uncorrelated to the S&P 500, until the Covid crisis hit and they lost three years of performance. The beta may have been low but the correlation significant enough to erode much of their gain.

Often hedge funds are lumped into this generic "alternatives" bucket, which mask what it is they are and why they are in the portfolio. It is sometimes assumed they are just uncorrelated sources of alpha, but many questions should be asked. It is not enough to analyze whether a fund seems attractive as a stand alone product, it needs to be understood in the context of the whole. Is this fund an equity surrogate, and will it contribute to the beta the portfolio needs to generate to meet a client's long term objective? Is it meant to diversify the return stream, and generate positive returns in all environments? Is it truly uncorrelated, or only steady in normal environments? When has it underperformed and what were the conditions? Is that likely to recur? Was performance driven by individuals who may leave?

Access to hedge funds is getting easier, as more funds are willing to open up to non-institutional investors and some are placed in a liquid mutual fund wrapper. Ease of access does not mean ease of analysis, however. They are complicated animals that often seek to denature the embedded risks. Some of these funds hyper-focus on statistical relationships or investment theory to control their risks and alpha opportunities. But putting the animal in a small cage does not make it more tame.

Some of the largest hedge funds have adopted an approach to multi-sector investing that deserves its own section. Not necessarily because of incredible performance, but because it is an interesting outlook on the investment opportunity available, and has influenced how I think about risk. This strategy is called **Risk Parity**, and has been described as an "all weather" strategy that will do well regardless of the economic environment.

Financial Advisors often suggest traditional allocations such as 60/40 portfolios (i.e. 60% stocks, 40% bonds) because historically this blend has had both respectable absolute returns and respectable risk-adjusted returns (i.e. a good Sharpe Ratio). Over the last few decades the bond allocation has effectively zigged while the market zagged while delivering performance as well. The future does not look like the past though. As we stare at 1.60bp yield on 10yr US Treasury Notes, the ability of bonds to deliver on price and income is no longer guaranteed. Advocates of Risk Parity also feel the 60/40 portfolio is flawed because a tremendous amount of the risk is coming from stocks because they have a significantly higher volatility. When the stock market collapses, all bonds can do is soften the blow; they can't counter the performance because they don't have enough volatility to generate an offsetting positive return.

Proponents of Risk Parity (in its pure form) believe that timing the market, or predicting which asset class will perform best at any moment is impossible to forecast. All those efficient frontier exercises aren't helpful if we really don't know what the actual return will be. For this reason, investors should own a bit of each compensated risk factors in such proportion *that its contribution to volatility is the same* – risk... parity. This would typically include all the compensated risk categories: equity, interest rates, credit, and inflation – but each practitioner of the strategy has their own approach.

A quick example of how risk parity works. As a starting place, let us assume a portfolio with 60% stocks and 40% bonds. We will assume 0 correlation of the stocks and bonds for simplicity.

	Weight	Expected Return	Volatility	Weighted Volatility
Stocks	60%	6.00%	19.50%	11.7%
Bonds	40%	4.00%	4.50%	1.8%
Portfolio		5.20%		13.50%

You will note that most of the risk (volatility) comes from stocks, as it has the higher weight and the higher level of volatility. You can also note that bonds are much more efficient in this case, given that an expected return of 4% only "costs" 5% of volatility, while an expected return of 6% comes with 19.5% volatility.

What does it look like if the stocks and bonds each contributed the same amount of risk? Since equities have 4.3x the volatility of bonds we solve for the bond allocation to be 81% and stocks 19% (rounded). The new portfolio looks like this:

	Weight	Expected Return	Volatility	Weighted Volatility
Stocks	18.8%	6%	20%	3.7%
Bonds	81.3%	4%	5%	3.7%
		4.38%		7.3%

Although the total return is lower by about 80bp, the Volatility is lower by 600bp. With this in hand we can target exactly the volatility we want. Suppose we target 10% volatility, to achieve this we need to introduce leverage (essentially negative cash), at a cost of let's say 2%.[42] To illustrate we add a third line called "Cash":

---

[42] By "cost" of leverage we mean the rate a prime broker charges an investor to borrow money to finance the levered position.

	Weight	Expected Return	Volatility	Weighted Volatility
Stocks	25.6%	6.0%	20%	5.0%
Bonds	111.1%	4.0%	5%	5.0%
Cash	-37%	2.0%		
	100.0%	5.25%		10.0%

In this scenario, we have managed to increase the expected return, while at the same time decreasing the volatility. This occurred because of the efficiency of the bond investment (higher Sharpe Ratio). The investor has also re-allocated **his risk** from a dominant equity position to an equal contribution from stocks and bonds. In reality, stocks and bonds may have a negative correlation, decreasing portfolio volatility further. Any number of risk classes can be added to the mix. It should be noted that the goal of risk parity is not necessarily an improved Sharpe Ratio but a portfolio with components that will perform in any market environment, with volatility scaled so that the in-favor asset class will have meaningful contribution to portfolio return.

Once the portfolio component proportions are derived, the investor can choose how much volatility she would like to target. The higher the volatility, the higher the expected return. Volatility is controlled by dialing up and down the amount of cash in the portfolio. Adding cash would douse the volatility, while maintaining negative cash (using leverage) would scale up the volatility.

There are many flaws with this strategy: First, volatility itself can be volatile. In our example we have assumed that volatility is a fixed number determined from (presumably) historical data. In reality, and especially during times of crisis, it is not as clean, and targeting volatility while volatility is volatile introduces some risk – for example the manager may adjust the allocations for short term volatility spikes, reducing exposure to the components and possibly missing out on a rally. Second, the use of leverage may cause exaggerated losses in some asset classes that force positions to be reduced at weak prices. The inclusion here is not meant as an endorsement of the strategy, but because it combines two elements of portfolio construction that I think are crucial.

I often ask financial advisors what they want their portfolio to *do*. Usually I get blank stares when I ask that question. Obviously you want the portfolio to rise in value as much as possible. But how do you describe your constraints? I want it to generate income. I want it to have low volatility. I want to have protection from inflation. Or simply I want it to grow as much as possible. It can be one thing or everything. But if you can't articulate what is happening in your portfolio, the portfolio won't respond well. And there is a difference between saying "I want to earn dividends" and "I need a 2.5% dividend yield". The two statements of intent can lead to very different portfolios.

The second questions I ask is "how do you intend to accomplish that?" There is no one right answer. But it should be thought out. Every component of the portfolio should be a building block towards those portfolio goals. If it's not furthering that goal it shouldn't be there. For example, if a prospect has a high degree of risk tolerance, but has a large allocation to cash, then either he is misleading you about his risk tolerance or he is misusing his cash.

What I love about risk parity is the concept clearly articulates a challenge and a solution: I want to create a portfolio that can generate returns in any economic environment. To accomplish that I weight my holdings in terms of their risk, so one market condition won't be more successful or weaker than another. And I target a specific volatility to reflect how much risk I am willing to bear.

When building your portfolios, this is an aesthetic you should aspire to: a very clear understanding of what you are trying to do and how you will accomplish that. Having this in mind makes your process easier to explain, and easier to defend.

At this point I want to review some guiding principles that we developed. These concepts do much of the heavy lifting for the portfolio construction process and it helps to summarize, to provide clarity of purpose and beliefs.

1. **We are able to invest in an efficient risk portfolio that delivers a superior return for a given amount of risk.** This core tenet of investing characterizes the investment decision as a question of whether each individual asset will enhance returns, or reduce risk. Although we cannot know in advance which assets will be dominant, our view of assets should be consistent client to client. Each client may have a different tolerance for risk, but the nature of the risk we do take should be similar.

2. **There is an appropriate beta, or market exposure we need to reach to deliver the clients goals.** Stock market beta will probably provide most of the returns over a client's lifetime. Of all the choices that impact returns, the choice to be invested in the market or not is likely to be dominant. It also helps you create a benchmark for success. Looking at raw return number is meaningless without a context to view it.

3. **There is a benchmark that we can build that incorporates our views on diversification and adheres to the client's constraints.** An explainable and justifiable benchmark should be monitored and understood by the investor and client. It could be fully elaborated with specific exposures to sub-asset classes, or it can be as simple as a percent allocated to a bond index and a percent allocated to a stock index. The advisor may have the same discretion in either circumstance, but evaluating the results depends on how you define the benchmark.

4. **Sharpe Ratios can help us understand our goals.** Though we want to maximize returns, we want to do so without introducing unnecessary volatility. When we look at incorporating new assets into the portfolio we should think about whether it offers diversification benefits or has a high probability of generating excess returns.

5. **We must not lose sight of our constraints.** A portfolio is built with a purpose from the ground up. Bolt on decisions made after the fact can introduce risks that have not been carefully vetted in the context of the entire portfolio. If undisciplined in our investment process the portfolio risk and attributes can easily drift from an initially well designed concept.

6. **We do not have a portfolio of good ideas, we have one portfolio that as a whole, is the best idea.** Not every position will work all the time. Emerging markets has phenomenal years sometimes, and then it underperforms. But to the extent it performs when other stock sectors are weak it provides a diversification benefit. We should look at the portfolio with pragmatism, as a solid, resilient product that can be trusted to behave if you close your eyes for a moment.

Hopefully these thoughts can help you develop portfolios that **express** your thoughts and motivations. An outsider should be able to understand what the goals and concerns are by viewing the components and the summary statistics. You should always be able to know what you're doing and what your intentions are, because you can't effectively change course without knowing where you're going!

PART FOUR: THE BUILDING BLOCKS
HOW YOU GET THERE – ALLOCATION AND ASSESSMENT

Thus far the only important decision has been deciding on a benchmark. That decision incorporates your strategic views of how much risk a client needs to maintain, and the granular decisions of how much geographic and asset class diversity is prudent. A simple benchmark of the S&P 500 index reflects a heightened risk preference as well as a narrow view of what represents the market. A complex benchmark that contains multiple equity and bond indices may serve a better purpose of expressing client needs and an investment worldview, but is more difficult to explain to clients, especially when sub-components are out of favor. For example, a stated exposure to international, small cap, and value stocks would have weighed heavily on a benchmark in recent years. If the client accepted the benchmark, then underperformance vs simple US large cap indexes would be irrelevant, because the manager in fact did not underperform his stated mission.

What the manager must defend is deviations from what he says he is going to do. I've seen many managers state an interest in comparing their portfolios' performances against the S&P 500 Index return, and then add mutual funds with a thumb in the air approach --   10% of this, 15% of that... until the portfolio is allocated. One year later the manager and client then look back and say "how did it go?".

This approach is not truly investing, certainly not as a professional endeavor. Sure, funds are allocated to risk for the purpose of realizing returns, but so is blindly picking mutual fund names from a hat. What makes investing rise to the level of a professional activity is having a purpose in each decision. I come back to this often and must reiterate: "What exactly are you trying to do?".

The first step is to know what is in the indices that make up your benchmark. For the equity portion of a portfolio, what kind of companies are included, how big are these companies, what sectors are they in, what countries are they in? For the fixed income portfolio of a portfolio, what are the credit ratings? When do maturities occur? What kind of structures are permitted?

These are your opportunities to generate alpha, and you have four options – neutral, overweight, underweight, or include "out of index" options.

These are the micro-decisions we are faced with. Which fund or stock we are adding to the portfolio is not the most important aspect of seeking alpha. The decision that matters is how are we positioned RELATIVE to the set of assets (our benchmark) that we consider a neutral position. If our benchmark is down 30% and our client is down 10%, then we can reasonably say that is a phenomenal result. If that is not good for the client, then the benchmark is wrong. Therefore, our decisions must be geared towards what outperforms the benchmark, not what outperforms zero.

As you build your clients' portfolio, the first thing to do is **make it look like your benchmark**, and then decide what you really like about it, and what you don't like about it presently – as a short-term active tactical decision – not as a long-term strategic decision. You are throwing puzzle pieces on the ground and just picking them back up, looking at them, and adding them back to the whole.

As the number of holdings grow, the individual relevance of specific holdings declines. Using the S&P 500 index as a benchmark would have approximately 500 components, though the largest ten could contribute a significant amount of performance. Using a broader index like the Russell 1000, Russell 3000, or S&P 1500 would flatten out those highest contributing stocks by market value.

We have discussed the benefits of diversification from a theoretical standpoint. Ideally, owning negatively- or low-correlated assets reduces your volatility with minimal reduction of return. Owning Boeing stock seems like a great idea, until it doesn't. Diversification minimizes the risk of specific stock picking, and lets us think more broadly about how to "beat the market" because picking the right stock is fraught with the unknown and unknowable.

Instead, let us compare the structure of our portfolio against that of our benchmark. To be clear, we do not mean looking at individual line items. What would we use? For stocks we could look at sector, or industry level allocation. We could look (for example) at company size allocation, from micro-cap to mega-cap. We could look at valuation metrics or growth metrics. For bond funds, we could look at duration, corporate vs government allocation, yield curve positioning, exposure to volatility. These are not meant to be comprehensive, whatever style or aesthetic you are reaching for is appropriate. What matters is whether you have the information and whether it is **controllable.**

Some institutional investors think in terms of **levers**, the specific risk exposures that are available and easy to control. For example, if you believe an appropriate benchmark should only include the stocks of US Large Capitalization companies, you could still control the average or median market value of your component companies. You could overweight technology and underweight consumer staples. The lever you are pulling is very specific. As you start with the index, you can pull the lever to increase the market value to make a bet on larger companies. You can pull the lever to overweight technology, and underweight consumer staples. You can also adjust your beta. <u>These are conscious decisions, not accidents.</u>

I worked with a financial advisor who loved investing in the health care sector, and he loved dividend stocks. The advisor used mutual funds for his stock exposure, with a number of dividend focused funds and a health care sector fund. But the dividend funds tended to have very low exposure to health care relative to his benchmark, so he was *underweight* a sector that he favored. And perhaps worse, he didn't know he was underweight.

Your tactical levers should be connected to an outlook that you are tracking on an ongoing basis. If you are not in control of the information basis for a trade, you may lose effectiveness from your trade. For example, if you believe inflation will be rising you may decide to replace nominal treasury bonds with TIPS. But TIPS yields imply a future inflation rate (the breakeven inflation rate). Adding them without being aware of the breakeven rate or not tracking the holding as the breakevens change will make the investment untargeted and aimless. Without control of our levers we can accumulate positions that seemed like a good idea on purchase that no longer make sense. Using levers carefully is not just a what (what am I trying to change), but a why (an explicit rationale). Ideally, it also includes a when (conditions when it makes sense to return to neutral).

It should be noted that your levers will be specific to your asset class. The methods you use to control an equity portfolio, or a multi-asset portfolio, will be different from your levers on a fixed income portfolio. Fixed income managers are much more concerned about the level of rates, the shape of the yield curve, exposure to credit risk, and volatility, among other risks. What is important is you track attributes that seem relevant and impactful for your investment process.

Your levers are like a sound mixing console -you adjust your guitar, your vocals, etc. Your levers are your exposure relative to the index. When you know where your levers are set, it is quite easy to track, and readjust. If on the other hand you are unsure of what your exposures are, how do you know how much to change? How do you know if you need to change? Without these controls you just have an unguided missile of a portfolio. You may weave and dodge, but invariably you are in a *reactive* posture.

The academic literature glided for awhile on the assumption that there was no way to consistently outperform and 'efficient markets' ruled. But the concept of efficient markets left room for some way to explain why some assets outperformed the market and others didn't. Embedded within the theory was an assumption that there was a pricing model that *would* explain such deviations. The earliest widely adopted model, the Capital Asset Pricing Model, explained differences in price returns as a simple function of how much beta an asset had relative to the market.

By the early 1990s, as computational power and data availability increased, the ability to test some of these assumptions became more widely available. One of the most important academic research papers on the subject was presented by Professors Eugene Fama and Kenneth French, in 1992. That seminal paper found that company size and value (relative cheapness) in addition to beta had explanatory power in asset returns – that is – you *could* beat the market by investing in small caps and less expensive stocks.[43] These are **factors** that have been found to statistically explain outperformance. Beta can be considered the first factor.

In statistics, a factor is an independent variable that is used by a statistical analyst to try to explain the movement in a test variable. In finance we are often trying to understand how some important concepts like interest rates and stock performance can be explained or predicted by other observable indicators. Even if there is poor prediction value, we may be able to tell when securities are mispriced if we have a well-defined "model" of the relationship. When the term "factor" is used in a portfolio context, it has a more loaded meaning because it is no longer a statistical experiment, but is used by some as a de facto attribute of outperformance.

---

[43] Explanatory power is a statistical term that indicates a theory has a demonstrated ability to explain an observed phenomenon. In this case statisticians and financial researchers are trying to understand and explain why some stocks have higher returns than others.

Andrew Berkin and Larry Swedroe describe conditions for successful factors in their book "Your Guide to Factor-Based Investing". A Factor should be:

- **Persistent** over time and **pervasive** across multiple markets
- **Robust** to various definitions (that is, tweaking the factor definition should not destroy the excess return)
- **Implementable**, still delivering alpha even after transaction costs.
- **Intuitive**, with a coherent reason for why the anomaly exists.

Factors may provide extra return because of economic reasons (value stocks are more closely aligned to intrinsic fundamentals; smaller stocks *should* outperform because they are inherently riskier, and need a higher equity premium) or behavioral reasons (momentum stocks capture something in the market psychology – a significant counter-argument to efficient markets hypothesis).

Though now there are hundreds of attributes considered factors (sometimes derisively referred to as the "factor zoo"), there are about six that are often tracked now: Momentum, Value, Quality, Low Volatility, Size, and Dividend Yield.

Factor	Definition
Value	Stocks which are inexpensive relative to fundamentals
Low Size	Companies with smaller market capitalization
Momentum	Securities displaying positive price trends
Quality	Companies with strong balance sheet and more stable earnings
Dividend Yield	Stocks with a high dividend relative to price
Low Volatility	Securities with low historical price volatility

Source: https://www.ishares.com/us/resources/tools/factor-box-resources#methodology

We can use mathematical expressions to describe sometimes qualitative attributes, making them comparable across companies. For example the Value factor may be represented by Price to Earnings, Price to Cash Flow, Price to Book, or dividend yield ratios. [44] The final Value score may be calculated as a combination of all the ratios, and statistical methods would be used to normalize

---

[44] Performance of the Value factor has been inconsistent lately. Although it was very strong in 2022 when growth stocks suffered, there is some concern that the increasing prevalence of intangible assets in corporate balance sheets is distorting the Value signal.

the range of values to provide a scale that allow for comparisons across companies, sectors, and concepts.[45] There is some subjectivity to how the factors for a stock are derived and scored – which ratios to include, how to combine them, and how to scale them - so different analytical tools may not return identical results.

There are many ETFs that can be mostly passive but *Tilt* a target benchmark index towards stocks that possess relatively more of these factor attributes, targeting just one factor or multiple factors at once. These funds are often described as **"Smart Beta"** – acknowledging the power of the market to efficiently allocate assets but ostensibly adding a bit more intelligence to the default market basket. The designer of the ETF specifies a benchmark according to rules that would express a preference for its targeted factor.

Reviewing actual factor exposures and reviewing methodology are very important in evaluating these funds. You may find a Value-oriented ETF has sacrificed a tremendous amount of the Momentum factor to achieve its goals. Meanwhile, a "multi-factor" fund that overweights stocks that have the highest value scores and separately the highest momentum scores (evaluated separately) will perform differently than a fund that overweights stocks with the highest average factor scores.

In an idealized investment world, every stock can be decomposed into its exposure to factors and we could describe any portfolio as the sum of its exposures to each factor.   Quantitative investors can be indifferent to the individual stocks and their stories.   The narrative they follow is a discrete, mathematical evaluation that can be observed and adjusted with precision. But we don't have to be zealots of the math to understand and use factor analysis.

---

[45] Data is normalized to enable comparisons of data series with vastly different ranges. We "normalize" data by scaling or adjusting a series - often to establish a range of values from 0 to 1 – in effect describing each data point as its distance from the minimum and maximum values. The meaning of differences in normalized data could be interpreted consistently. If we were testing a statistical hypothesis, the coefficients would have the same scale regardless of which series was being examined, and higher and lower values would imply the same higher and lower sensitivity to the normalized factor.

At the individual stock level there is little that can be said about the nature of the entire portfolio. However, analyzing a portfolio's sensitivity to factors, its so-called **"factor loading"**, provides measurable and controllable levers that augments a manager's ability to fine tune a portfolio's risk. Financial advisors can use tools like Blackrock 360 to compare their portfolio's factor profile against global indexes, or use subscription services like Morningstar Direct to see a detailed, granular breakdown of factor exposure. Either through directly using smart beta ETFs or mutual funds, or calibrating with a portfolio analysis tool, factors have become another lever that can be used to tilt portfolios toward a preferred balance. Those tilts can be a permanent profile that seeks to profit from the factors' long-term outperformance potential, or a timing strategy that favors different factors depending on economic conditions.

Factors can also be used to measure risk broadly. Thus far the discussion has centered on narrowly defined *rewarded* factors that research has found to outperform. Much marketing of smart beta products implies that the only factors are those that have been found to generate excess returns. However, there is an immense library of broadly categorized *risk* factors with economic significance that helps understand risk exposures in more complex ways.

Invesco describes the advantages of using factor analysis for risk management: "(it) identifies the key underlying drivers of risk and performance across securities, sectors, and asset classes. This approach allows us to untangle often-complex relationships across investments that influence performance in a portfolio. Is performance tightly linked to equity market performance or economic growth? Is it affected by inflation? Is it sensitive to changes in interest rates? Factor analysis narrows the scope of risk analysis from a nearly unlimited pool of individual investments to a finite list of factors that describe their behavior."[46]

We could say that correlation with the price of oil is a factor, or investment in research and development, or sensitivity to interest rates. There are risk models that would analyze a portfolio across thousands of factors to tease out difficult to discover relationships. Large institutional investors with multiple asset classes

---

[46] Invesco Investment Solutions Focus Paper Series: Factors for Risk Management

and investment vehicles can crunch their portfolio to discover vulnerabilities that would be invisible without a sophisticated factor model.

When we use factors to invest we are stripping the names and narrative away from individual securities. We care less about an exciting new company, and more about sales growth. Less about the financial strength of one company and more about strong balance sheets generally. While this process loses nuance it may gain consistency and control.

Factor outperformance has been discovered and reaffirmed many times since the first academic papers on the subject, though "proven" is a harder standard. The performance in the real world market has often disappointed investors who had been impressed by paper portfolios in the research. Some factors seem to be more persistent across different markets, some factors have more robust statistical confidence. Other factors vacillate between significance and noise but improve when the data is adjusted. For example, the size factor can falter, but when unprofitable small companies are excluded from the sample the test becomes stronger. Some factors work much better in combination with others. The results of these papers are affected by the method of testing, look back period, and inclusion universe - and can be vulnerable to data mining. A thorough digest of the literature is beyond the scope of this work. Further investigation is encouraged.

In early discussions of the benefits of diversification, an ideal scenario was introduced — where two assets were negatively correlated but each still had a positive expected return. Any opportunity to introduce low correlations helped a portfolio skip up the efficient frontier — less risk for the same expected return. Most of the time there was at least some positive correlation — US equities may not be perfectly correlated with world markets but the correlation is still high. Factors can offer a unique diversification opportunity because not only are returns expected to outpace the market (beta), the correlations between some factor are low and negative! Not every factor will work all the time, but exposure to each (or as many as possible) in above market loadings can theoretically provide a higher baseline return with lower risk.

In Vanguard's publication "Equity factor-based investing: A practitioner's guide", a correlation matrix is published that illustrates the factors return relationship to each other.

It would make sense that Value and Quality would have negative correlations (-.59) — if Value stocks (which are often somewhat distressed which causes shares to cheapen) are doing well, it would be inconsistent for Quality stocks to outperform as well. If the literature is correct, the market rewards both factors

– but at different times. Owning both offers the chance of outperformance regardless of the market regime.

Correlation of monthly excess returns: 2002–2016

	Value	Quality	Volatility	Momentum	Size	Liquidity
Value						
Quality	−0.59					
Volatility	−0.38	0.49				
Momentum	−0.11	0.37	0.37			
Size	0.43	−0.30	−0.15	0.10		
Liquidity	0.57	−0.44	−0.13	0.08	0.63	

■ High: > 0.7   ■ Medium: 0.3–0.7   ■ Low: < 0.3

Notes: Data cover 31 December 2001 through 30 September 2016. Excess returns are calculated relative to the MSCI World Total Return Index (USD).
Sources: Vanguard calculations, using data from Thomson Reuters Datastream, MSCI, Bloomberg, and FTSE.

As already stated, some factors perform well at the same time others are unfavored. This creates an opportunity for factor timing for more tactical-oriented portfolio managers. Knowing where we are in the market cycle can inform which factors to push harder on. MSCI has published research on average monthly factor return performance in specific economic conditions: Recovery, Expansion, Slowdown, and Contraction. Knowing or anticipating the business phase can inform your Factor loading.

Factors can also be evaluated based on their valuation, similar in concept to looking at P/E ratios for individual sectors. Some research has found Factors that are cheaper (compared to their historical averages) can outperform. It has also been found that factors themselves have momentum – a factor that has been in favor may remain in favor.

None of this is easy. Though investing efforts are buttressed by the enormous amount of research devoted to Factors, it guarantees nothing. For portfolio managers who devote their method to these concepts, it is a calming True North. To those who are cognizant of their factor positioning, it is a useful guiding light. Factors are a risk like any other, though harder to track and trade. Using them provides more insight – ignoring them does not make the risk go away.

114

Many financial advisors, when taking on new clients with already invested portfolios, see the client's existing positions as a problem with one solution – liquidating the entire portfolio and reinvesting into the new advisor's model. For tax deferred or tax exempt accounts that is usually not problematic (except for bid/ask spread and market timing slippage), but for taxable accounts it can lead to huge realized gains and tax consequences. Another approach is for the advisor to take a hands off approach, and hold legacy positions with large gains separately and unmanaged from the rest of the portfolio. Direct Indexing may also be used to transition the portfolio over time if the client had sufficient assets to qualify. If the advisor was more aware of his levers, it is a more addressable problem.[47]

The portfolio should represent your worldview, and the levers are the expression of it. Any stock portfolio probably has significant overlap to your benchmark index. Shedding an entire portfolio to rebuy the same stocks (within different funds) is a wasteful exercise. What matters are the active bets you wish to make with respect to that index. Selling one dividend fund and buying another with the same mandate isn't a necessary change. What is important is leaning into the levers that matter to you and pulling back on those for which you disagree. From the top looking down, without looking at the individual line items, does the new portfolio reflect your view of the world?

To begin making active bets the manager needs to start thinking about what levers are to be pulled, and how far to pull them. For that we need data. Morningstar has pioneered the analysis of mutual funds and has developed some of the earliest ways to quickly evaluate what is packaged inside. Their methodology and research tools are as applicable when examining entire portfolios.

---

[47] At some point massive capital gains cannot be mitigated, and a detailed client conversation needs to take place addressing either a taxable gain tolerance or an acknowledgement that securities and positions are not a long-term recommended hold from the advisor's perspective. Also, the direct indexing approach implicitly incorporates many of the themes in this chapter as the statistical sampling process essentially captures the dominant levers in the advisor's model, whether the advisor has recognized them or not.

Within equity portfolios, the most basic levers to pull are the size and style metrics. One of the first tools to evaluate an equity allocation is the Style Box, introduced in 1992 (coincidentally when Fama and French first wrote about Factor returns). The Style Box shows in an easy-to-read 3x3 matrix with the vertical axis representing Market Capitalization (i.e. Large-Cap, Mid-Cap, and Small-Cap) and the horizontal axis representing Style (i.e. Value, Growth, and "Blend).[48] Each of the nine boxes hence represent the percentage of the portfolio by market capitalization that is held in a certain category of company (E.g large-

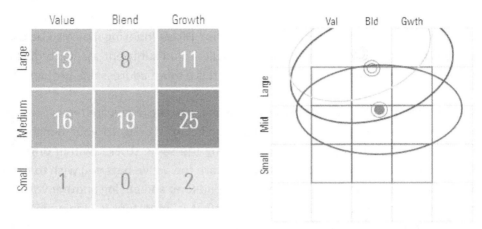

cap growth, small-cap blend). The numbers in the box typically total to 100%, though rounding can cause the boxes to not sum correctly.

These boxes neatly show where a portfolio's stock exposure is allocated. The first box pictured above shows in basic percentages what the allocation is, while the second box gives a more comprehensive view of the diversity of the allocation and a quick comparison with similar funds and a benchmark. In this case we can quickly see that this fund has a heavier weight to mid-cap stocks compared to similar portfolios.

As mentioned previously, another common lever is sector allocation. Though no sector has historically presented regular outperformance that cannot be explained by other factors, at any moment, given relative valuation or

---

[48] Blend stocks are those companies that are dominated by neither growth or Value attributes.

macroeconomic fundaments we may choose to have higher weights to preferred sectors, or avoid others. Our choice of sectors may indicate our preference for safety (consumer staples) or income (utilities) or interest rate direction (financials and real estate), or robust economic expansion (consumer discretionary, technology, industrials). We can also use valuation metrics to compare sectors against each other, or compared to where they have historically been priced relative to each other.

Any metric that can be tracked can be used as a lever, operated just by moving the allocations up or down *relative to the index.* Some are more powerful than others, requiring very little movement to be effective. Beta for example, is easy to change and incredibly impactful. After twenty years, the benefits of being overweight growth or value will probably be small but changing the beta of a portfolio could be very consequential.

Factors can also be used as levers. Though harder to track and more difficult to control without a third- party analysis model, the portfolio can be tilted towards preferred factors, or even all of them. You may want to know that your overall exposure to Momentum or Quality is higher than that of the market baseline. For individual funds you can see the factor exposure profile on Morningstar's website.

When I was young my sister asked me if I could stick out my tongue and touch the tip of my nose. I tried mightily but couldn't do it. She then stuck her tongue out and touched her nose with her finger. Investing has similar lessons. You don't need a single solution to design what you need. You will find that if your levers are well-defined, you can build ways to directly access them within the portfolio. While you may have your favorite allocations that you believe generate alpha, you can also have specific funds that you can toggle up and down to change the portfolio profile. Small cap to large cap, quality to momentum, sector funds – any concept of lever you want to control could have a dedicated fund to do that. We tend to gravitate towards diversified funds for the safety and risk mitigation properties they offer. We may be wary of single theme investments because of the risk of being wrong. But as a small part of your larger portfolio it gives you the dexterity to reposition with ease. You don't have to think about how to change, the mechanism is already there, the lever is already labeled.

Levers can also be used for portfolio efficiency. If you are targeting specific active positions against a benchmark, the bulk of the portfolio can be a low-fee fund that mirrors the benchmark itself. Targeted ETFs or mutual funds can be used to achieve very specific expressions of your desired levers. This creates a very controllable, and very inexpensive portfolio. It also saves time as you have less concern for correlations and overlapping holdings or exposures between your satellite investments.

Returning to the example of an advisor inheriting a portfolio with large unrealized gains, instead of liquidating the advisor can adjust the portfolio to reflect the levers he feels are important to pull. As we are less concerned with individual fund names, we can now concentrate on the risks we want to express. There is no need to sell a large number of stocks (within the funds) most of which would likely be re-purchased in a different vehicle. One can argue that it forces the manager to own funds and assets he does not know and has not researched, but he should have a due diligence process.

Of course not everything needs to be controlled, and you may not have a particular view. But if you do not have a view, do not take a position! These decisions are not just thumb in the air choices, and should never be accidental.

Toggle Positions

One of the biggest complications of managing portfolios for private wealth clients is the heterogeneity that naturally occurs in the portfolios. Some managers may have hundreds of different accounts with different levels of embedded capital gains, legacy assets that were incorporated rather than replaced, tax loss harvesting substitutes that were maintained in taxable accounts, or any other reasonable explanation for drift away from the standard current investment model. This makes adjustment of your Levers in a quick and automated manner across clients difficult. If you decided to reduce position X by 50% and give orders to the trader, it might not have the same risk impact for all.

When we are constructing our models for broad client use, it is crucial to know from the top down how our Levers are set relative to the benchmark. But we should also be mindful of how, from a practical standpoint, we will adjust the levers when needed. If the portfolio is made of individual stocks, the adjustment may involve a large number of small trades. If the portfolio is composed of broad market funds with only a mild bias towards a Lever, the impact may be too difficult to express, or the size in the portfolio so large that unneeded taxable gains would be realized.

For this reason, it is helpful to leave in the portfolio line items that are deliberately placed and sized to represent an expression of a Lever. For example, if a portfolio manager intended to make tactical decisions corresponding to 5% of the portfolio, he could identify a fund that would always represent the current emphasis, regardless of the manner in which the rest of the portfolio was invested. A transition of large-cap to small cap could easily be executed with a single switch of a pre-identified position. Or having the capability of moving between Value and Growth, or Domestic and International, or Quality Factor to Momentum. Ideally these positions would be placed in a non-taxable account so the transactions can occur without tax considerations, but that is not always available.

What is important is these "Toggle positions" are a concentrated, efficient exposure to the risk element you want to add or subtract from the portfolio. Having them with the purpose of tactical decision making in mind helps you evaluate and use your levers decisively, act quickly, keep client experience consistent, and maintain a strategic core of the portfolio that can remain intact regardless of the economic environment.

	Portfolio %	Bmark %
→ Defen	23.11	24.59
Cons Defensive	8.13	8.43
Healthcare	11.17	12.95
Utilities	3.81	3.21
∿ Sens	47.32	41.95
Comm Svcs	10.43	10.00
Energy	2.73	3.36
Industrials	11.41	9.25
Technology	22.75	19.34
↻ Cycl	29.57	33.47
Basic Matls	4.42	4.56
Cons Cyclical	10.69	11.24
Financial Svcs	11.89	14.70
Real Estate	2.57	2.97
Not Classified	0.00	-0.01

Valuation Multiples	Portfolio	B-mark
Price/Earnings	19.56	20.96
Price/Book	2.35	2.30
Price/Sales	1.29	1.73
Price/Cash Flow	10.26	11.84

Profitability

% of Stocks	2018	Portfolio 2019	B-mark 2019
Net Margin	13.89	14.21	16.00
ROE	20.65	21.01	21.00
ROA	7.33	7.26	7.00
Debt/Capital	38.64	40.72	40.00

Levers can be anything you can monitor and control. The Style Box is the most common breakdown of portfolio attributes but any metric can be targeted, some more readily than others. Portfolios should be created embedded with funds that can easily be shifted between concepts. This reduces the time it takes to react to a changing world. When you already know what your levers are, how they are set, and how to adjust them, portfolios can be managed at the speed of your market research.

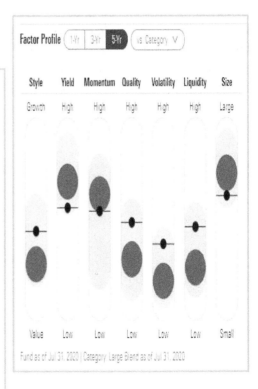

Factor Profile 1-Yr 3-Yr 5-Yr vs Category

Style	Yield	Momentum	Quality	Volatility	Liquidity	Size
Growth	High	High	High	High	High	Large
Value	Low	Low	Low	Low	Low	Small

Fund as of Jul 31, 2020 | Category Large Blend as of Jul 31, 2020

Benchmarks are a mental target that allows a portfolio manager to gauge what she's doing. Without having a target there would be no alpha. As fewer advisors beat the benchmarks, performance is deemphasized. I once read in a financial advisor newsletter an author stating baldly that generating alpha is not his concern, it's the burden of the fund managers he invests with. That is an absurd idea. *Unless you are investing passively in a benchmark you are taking active bets, and you are responsible for them!*

Another way to direct clients is by advocating a "goals-based investing" approach, where success is measured by how well a client progresses towards achieving specific life financial goals. There is nothing wrong with apportioning investment funds with different horizons for specific needs. However, if the road you take to get there (the client's portfolio) deviates from the way you said you'd get there (the benchmark) an explanation is in order, as well as an auditing.

Financial advisors need benchmarks simply for the feedback mechanism of knowing something is going wrong. How would we know if a mutual fund manager made some mistakes, and is taking outsized bets to recover performance? How would we know if an overweight in energy stocks caused by a high dividend bias is hurting performance? We can't use semantics to pretend financial goal achievement equals investment management excellence. They are two separate things. **It matters how much risk you took to achieve a goal.** If the portfolio returned 5%, that would be great if you had a low volatility bond strategy, but may be horrible if you were 100% invested in stocks and the market returned 20%. It doesn't matter if the client can now buy a boat if you took too much risk and had paltry returns. Conflating the goal with the performance disguises the skill of the investor.

That is why the benchmark is important. The benchmark is an unbiased arbiter of performance. To mirror the benchmark is to be passive – any deviation is an active bet, **deliberate or not**. Investing in passive funds, but weighted to diverge from the benchmark, remains an active allocation that can affect relative performance, and how you are evaluated.

This does not mean there is only one way to look at the world, one index that explains *your* strategy. Simple, single index benchmarks may be sufficient, and any deviation in your portfolios can be alpha. The identical portfolio that is perfectly matched against a complex benchmark of multiple indices will generate no alpha – all performance would simply be beta – your exposure to systematic risk and your benchmark.

For example, many financial advisors use the MSCI All Country World Index (ACWI) because it is a broad, global index. Over 40% of the index consists of non-US companies. An advisor could certainly hug the index, keeping close to that international allocation. Alternatively, if an advisor believes that 40% is too high and permanently (strategically, as opposed to tactically) aim for 20%, there are two choices.

One can keep the ACWI benchmark, and the underweight to international stocks is an active bet that will generate alpha, positive or negative. Or one can create a custom benchmark made of perhaps 80% Vanguard Total Stock Market and 20% MSCI EAFE (Europe, Australasia, and the Far East) or ACWI excluding US stocks, or any other global non-US index. In this situation the allocation to international stocks is a benchmark weight, and not a deliberate tactical bet.

Why would you choose one approach or the other? Having a simple, single index benchmark is straightforward and easy to explain to clients. And if your deviations from the benchmark generate better returns you appear to have added value to the client. Having a complex benchmark accurately reflects how you plan to invest their funds. Many clients are not paying attention to the nuance of your benchmark, until they've noticed you've underperformed what they had in mind.

You do not have to take bets, to always be trying to outperform. If you have a clear vision of an ideal passive allocation that may never change, and you can explain that to clients, your benchmark can be your portfolio. But active bets are purposeful – and they **are** your deliverable.

So you've decided on a benchmark, you have some levers. Some investors may start rubbing their hands together and start looking for mutual funds and stocks with great track records, but you still need to go slow.

Look at the components of your benchmark, look at the summary statistics (P/E Ratios, revenue growth, leverage ratios, etc.). Decide what aspects of it you like and don't like *right now.*   A simple example – historically value stocks have outperformed growth stocks, but over the last few years, growth stock performance has trounced value stocks. We may not want to create a new benchmark to reflect a permanent aversion to value, but for the moment we may want to overweight growth stocks.

Let's assume the S&P 500 was our benchmark. Here is a representative Style Box.

	Value	Blend	Growth
Large	28	30	28
Medium	5	4	2
Small	0	0	0

I want to be overweight growth, but how much? I've found that the answer to that question depends most on *how much you are willing to lose if you're wrong!* It's easy to get giddy about how much alpha you are going to make and how stupid everyone else in the market is. The reality is that maybe you are not as prescient as you think, and could be wrong. How do we go about thinking about this one trade? We need to make a number of statements.

First, we need to be specific about the bet being made: Large Cap Growth will beat Large Cap Value. Second, let us stipulate that we'd rather not lose more than 1% of alpha. We do not know what will happen in advance. The best indication we have of what could happen is what has happened in the past.

Let's use two index-based ETFs, the Vanguard Value ETF (VTV) and Vanguard Growth ETF (VUG) to illustrate how this trade has historically performed[49]. Here we are examining annual returns going back to 2005 (readily available from Yahoo Finance). We see that on average Growth has outperformed Value by about 4.5%. However, we really don't know whether that trend will continue and there is no precedent to assume it will. Historically, over decades, Value has outperformed. But let's assume the expected return of this trade is zero. We can also calculate that one standard deviation of the relative performance is 12% and that seems like a reasonable approximation of the risk of this trade. We have approximately two thirds chance (one standard deviation) of being right or wrong on this trade by 12% of return. What if we were wrong?

---

[49] Ideally we use as much historical data as is available. This example uses ETFs as a proxy but the history is limited. There are many other sources available for a growth vs value analysis. The purpose here is to show an easy way to find and retrieve information that can inform how volatile a trade may be. It is likely not sufficient to back-test a trading strategy.

	Annual Returns		
	Value	Growth	Difference
2020	2.23%	40.16%	37.93%
2019	25.85%	37.26%	11.41%
2018	-5.39%	-3.32%	2.07%
2017	17.12%	27.80%	10.68%
2016	16.88%	6.13%	-10.75%
2015	-0.89%	3.32%	4.21%
2014	13.19%	13.62%	0.43%
2013	33.03%	32.38%	-0.65%
2012	15.19%	17.03%	1.84%
2011	1.16%	1.87%	0.71%
2010	14.45%	17.11%	2.66%
2009	19.72%	36.46%	16.74%
2008	-35.91%	-38.22%	-2.31%
2007	0.20%	12.68%	12.48%
2006	22.28%	9.13%	-13.15%
2005	7.19%	5.20%	-1.99%
	Standard Deviation		12%
	Average		4.52%

If we do not want to lose more than 1% of alpha for a one standard deviation move, simple algebra shows us how big this trade should be: 1% = (weight of trade) X 12% -- therefore we should have 8.3% (1% / 12%) more of the portfolio allocated to growth stocks than value stocks relative to the index. If value outperforms growth by 12%, the portfolio will underperform the index by 1%.[50]

Looking at the data, the difference in returns between growth and value seem to have a number of years with severe performance dislocations, and perhaps assuming a two standard deviation relative return difference may be more prudent. If we were then afraid of a two standard deviation move the equation would look like this: 1% = (weight of trade) X 24% -- and the relative weight should be 4.2%

---

[50] Note that the absolute difference in weight should be 8%, not 8% more or less than the current weight.

We can also use this technique to evaluate whether a trade's positioning is large enough to matter. We may choose small trades that seem like incrementally good ideas but if the deviation from a baseline is not sufficient enough to impact portfolio returns, the research effort and extra portfolio complexity may not be worthwhile. If a trade is worthy of investing in, it should be large enough to have a measurable impact.

The levers we pull that can be directly proxied by targeted ETFs provide much information and help us navigate our risk. ETFs can be found for individual sectors, global markets, and specific market capitalization segments. That said, not everything can be measured so explicitly. However, you will find that as you move your more impactful levers, you may lose control of smaller details. For example, choosing an overweight to growth will make it very hard to keep exposure to the Value factor high. There is a constant give-and-take that must be navigated.

It should be noted this is not an exact science. In an ideal world we have much more data that always correlates with the trade you are trying to make. However, we are trying to ballpark risk to know how much deviation from benchmark we are comfortable with from a probability of loss (underperformance) standpoint. For example, the performance of the Industrials sector correlates much more with that of the overall S&P 500 Index than does the Energy sector, which is dominated by economics specific to that sector. Therefore, the deviation in allocation weight to Industrials can be much higher than a deviation for the Energy sector.

Once you have decided on your benchmark, levers, and position sizes – it is finally time to fill in the blanks. At this point it is a very iterative process, as adding successive mutual funds or ETFs becomes harder, as each of their active positions begins to push against your boundaries. You will find that each adjustment requires a new portfolio recalculation, examining both your main levers weightings and how your factor positioning looks. It may be that an addition you really like may simply not fit. That's ok, as your portfolio is not a collection of line items, but a collection of risks that you are comfortable owning. Hold to your portfolio construction process. You have to remember that the portfolio is your end result, not any individual holding.

PART FIVE: MONITORING AND REPORTING
RETURN ATTRIBUTION AND MONITORING

It would be nice if an investor had a ten-year time horizon after which you could digest what happened, and all the good trades offset the bad trades, and on net you come out ahead through some contribution of factor loadings or skill. Hopefully it all plays out in the end. With a well-defined benchmark and only slight deviations, there may not be that much to say.

But if there are deviations from the plan from what you said you were going to do, at what point do you gauge the success of your efforts? Do you wait until year end to look at your alpha? Do you glance at client statements in preparation for a quarterly meeting? Or do you have a daily recap on your trade results to inundate you with real time data?

You clearly do not want to be hyper, and react to every bit of information. What is crucial though is being able to *get* your information on demand. If a financial advisor is looking at model portfolio returns and doesn't understand what happened, he may be ineffective as a manager of assets. If an advisor is taking active bets, the results of those bets should be accessible without having to create the metrics of discovery from scratch.

A simple return contribution analysis would say Asset x is y% of the portfolio and had a return of z%. The contribution of return for asset x is y * z. This is only meaningful if your benchmark return is zero. When comparing to an index this methodology is insufficient because the index *also* includes asset x. Now what matters is the *relative* weight of the asset in the portfolio.

If your portfolio is neatly allocated with a specific fund representing a specific sector, it is easy to gauge the impact. Let's say you have one Emerging Markets (EM) fund and allocated to the same percentage as your benchmark's exposure to EM. In this case the impact is easy to derive – it is simply the outperformance times the weight of the fund. If your EM fund outperformed the benchmark's EM stocks by 10%, and its weighting was 5% of your portfolio (and the benchmark) then your choice of EM fund added 50bp of alpha.[51] Analysis is more complicated when a fund straddles many different categories, and when your allocations deviate from benchmark.

When examining an entire portfolio's return we need to think about the bets we are taking, possibly in terms of our levers. In its simplest form we could define the performance of a single Sector X according to this formula:

$$(\text{Weight of } X_{portfolio} - \text{Weight of } X_{Index})* \text{Return}_{(Sector X)}$$

The limitation is that if we are overweight one asset, we *must* be underweight another asset. Whether it is an explicit trade or not, it is insufficient to find the true impact of an index mis-match this way. We also do not know the impact of our security selection.

A more thorough analysis is called **Return Attribution**, a two step process which looks at returns for each sector of a portfolio and compares it to index weight and index returns, and separately returns for each security in those sectors in the portfolio, and compares it to the index returns *for that sector*.

In this analysis the term "sector" is not necessarily meant as an industrial sector, but as a portfolio segmentation that meaningfully describes some aspect of its composition. Ideally the sectors are broken down by your levers, or separate return attribution calculations can be created breaking down the portfolio returns through a different lens. For example, we may want to look at returns based on industrial sector allocation, OR we may want to look at returns based on geographic location. Looking at both simultaneously may be too granular or difficult, yet both lenses provide information.

To be comprehensive and audit performance down to the basis point, you need complete data that represents the returns for all holdings found in the portfolio and the underlying index and an accounting of all the trades that occurred during

---

[51] As will be discussed, your decision to invest in EM stocks did not add alpha because it was already in the index at the same allocation. What matters in this case is the relative performance of the specific EM stocks you owned, not the sector level choice.

the period. But a less than perfect approach may be adequate for providing the information you need.

For example, let us use the Global Industry Classification Standard (GICS) as sectors of a hypothetical index and portfolio, with allocations and a set of returns:

Sector	Index Weight	Portfolio Weight	Difference (a)	Returns (b)	Sector Attribution
Communication services	11%	16%	5%	3.0%	-0.16%
Consumer discretionary	5%	8%	3%	5.4%	-0.03%
Consumer staples	20%	6%	-14%	9.2%	-0.40%
Energy	2%	14%	12%	4.2%	-0.24%
Financials	4%	1%	-2%	5.0%	0.03%
Health care	14%	4%	-11%	6.4%	-0.01%
Industrials	7%	15%	8%	1.6%	-0.38%
Information technology	13%	7%	-6%	6.4%	-0.01%
Materials	7%	14%	7%	7.3%	0.07%
Real estate	4%	9%	5%	5.3%	-0.05%
Utilities	13%	6%	-7%	7.7%	-0.11%
Total	100%	100%	0%		-1.29%

Portfolio Return: 5.01%
Index Returns: 6.30% (c)

For each sector we multiply the relative weight in the portfolio (a) by the difference between that sector's return and the return of the index (b-c). This calculation tells us the value of the decision to overweight and underweight each sector.

Let's look at an example. Suppose we want to see how our weighting decision of the Industrials sector fared. From the table we can see that the index had a total return of +6.3%, and the Industrials sector had a total return of 1.6%. Therefore, the Industrials sector *under*performed by 4.7%. Any manager who allocated to the Industrials sector *less* than the index would have added alpha, and vice versa. In this case, the index weight is 7% and our weight is 15%. Hence the portfolio lost alpha because of that decision. How much? We multiply the overweight of the industrials sector (15% - 7% = 8%) times the relative performance (1.6% - 6.3% = -4.7%) = .38% or 38 basis points.

To precisely calculate the sector returns you must know the returns of all the securities in the index and their proportion within each sector. This requires having access to pricing data and some spreadsheet work to maintain the return attribution model's accuracy. Without this information, a back of the envelope calculation is still possible using ETF proxies. For example, the Vanguard sector ETFs are not identical to the components of the S&P 500 Index, but their returns can be a reasonable substitute for relative sector performance. You retain information about how your sector choices are performing, but the net results will not perfectly capture the attribution.

In this example, the net difference in the sector returns perfectly equals the difference in return between the portfolio and the index. This is extremely unlikely. For this to occur the securities that make up each sector in the portfolio and index must be identical and held in the same proportion. The second layer of return attribution determines the contribution of the securities *within* the sector to the overall alpha.

To calculate the security specific contribution, for each security we would multiply the absolute weight of that security by the return of that security minus that sector's index return. In formula terms:

Security Specific Contribution = (Weight $_{\text{Security I}}$) x (Return $_{\text{Security I}}$ – Return $_{\text{Index Sector}}$)

Let's apply this to a specific stock. Consider this: At this beginning of the analysis period a portfolio holds Apple (AAPL) stock with an allocation of 3%. AAPL returns +80% during that period. The Technology sector has a return of +30% during that period.

AAPL has outperformed its sector by 50%. Because AAPL had an allocation of 3% in the portfolio, its security-specific contribution is thus 50% x 3% = 1.5% or 150bp. Of course the stocks you owned that underperformed the tech sector would detract from performance.

Sometimes it may not seem like we are making security selection biases in our investment allocation, but it may become apparent upon an annual post mortem. For example, in 2021 the Vanguard Technology sector ETF returned ~+30%. You may assume that an overweight to technology shares would have led to outperformance. But so-called "innovative" technology stocks experienced declines, with some targeted funds *down* over 10% for the year (following an exceptionally strong 2020). If your security mix contained an overweight to the "wrong" kind of technology it would depress your returns.

The combination of sector attribution and security level contribution provides important information. With complete data the two components create a thorough mathematical accounting of performance.[52] We can better understand the impact of our tactical decisions, as well as the quality of our vetting and due diligence of individual securities to express those views.

Unfortunately, when you invest in mutual funds you usually don't have a complete holdings list to create a fully elaborated Return Attribution. Furthermore, when you have mutual funds with exposures that overlap many of your sectors, security specific evaluation is not possible, as you cannot tease out which funds would be applied to which sector. For example, a broad allocation mutual fund straddles large cap stocks to small cap stocks, and value to growth allocations. This limitation, however, doesn't mean the exercise has no value.

Losing security specific return attribution metrics does not negate the value of the effort because we are focused on evaluating how our levers are functioning. Suppose a portfolio has these four positions relative to an index:

1. Overweight to Large Cap Growth
2. Underweight to Small Cap Value
3. Underweight to International stocks
4. Overweight to the Technology sector

These positions do not cleanly line up as sectors – two are size and style characteristics, one is a GICS sector, and one is a geographic differentiation. All of these may have overlapping effects – the overweight to technology may be partly due to an underweight in international stocks and you may be double counting the effect. While this may not be perfect, losing precision is better than having none at all.

---

[52] A complete and accurate calculation of return attribution would need to include security transactions that occurred during the period under review.

We can set up proxies for each of our discrete active positions and compare to our benchmark's returns. Lets say these are our biggest active positions:

Category	Relative Weight	Proxy
US Large Cap Growth	5%	Vanguard Growth ETF (VUG)
US Small Cap Value	-5%	Vanguard Small-Cap Value ETF (VBR)
US Technology	5%	Vanguard Information Technology ETF (VGT)
Non-US International	-5%	SPDR MSCI ACWI ex-US ETF (CWI)

With a clinical definition of our levers we can create a *back of the envelope* attribution. We use the same approach as the sector analysis. The performance of each lever compared to the index, multiplied by the relative weight verses the index. Even though we are not comprehensive, we can now point to a decision (a relative overweight) and an outcome.

	Return	Relative Weight	Impact
Benchmark Return	8%	--	--
Large Cap Growth	10%	5%	0.10%
Small Cap Value	6%	-5%	0.20%
Technology	12%	5%	0.30%
Non-US International	-5%	-5%	0.85%
Sector Effect Return Attribution			1.45%

With this methodology we have an idea of what worked, even acknowledging that the Large Cap Growth overweight and the Technology overweight would have some overlap. Ideally we have more information to fully elaborate the return attribution, but even imperfect reports can provide crucial feedback.

The benchmark in this scenario returned 8% and we have calculated that we could have outperformed by 145bp, or a 9.45% total performance (8% benchmark + 1.45% extra return from good sector selection). If the portfolio in this scenario returned only 9% (45bp less than calculated) we have an idea there were some other minor factors at play, or the discrepancy was caused by our imperfect attribution. If however, the portfolio returned 7% (a 100bp miss from the benchmark and far below our expectations), then our understanding of what is driving this portfolio's return is deeply flawed.

The frame and process we use to monitor return attribution also colors the results. For example, let's use an Equal Weighted S&P 500 Index ETF as one of our portfolio funds. Over some historical ranges these funds have outperformed the S&P 500 Index. But we actually have a choice in how we evaluate performance. Through one lens we can expect this fund to generate alpha, and compare its returns to the S&P 500 Index, *an analysis of security selection*. Or we can step back and say at the portfolio level, the components of the Equal-Weighted fund result in higher weights to mid-cap and value stocks, and the return captures the **sector level** impact of that positioning.

Every security or fund in a portfolio should be added with an understanding of its marginal effect on the portfolio balance, and have an idea how it will be evaluated. Otherwise, how do you know when it is underperforming and needs attention? You have to know in advance what you expect it to do.

The discussion here is meant to link the monitoring of portfolio performance with respect to the specific decisions you make – pulling levers and tracking the results. Even without sophisticated analytical tools, we can make progress with some basic algebra. However, if one has access to more sophisticated resources, the data can be quite helpful.

Services such as Morningstar Direct can create detailed Return Attribution report calculated using any lens that is useful to your process. One can use GICS sector allocation, or factor loading, or geographic diversification to evaluate performance. More is better (provided the user isn't overwhelmed and incapable of digesting the results), but even rudimentary models and Excel spreadsheets are better than nothing.

It should also be noted that we are as likely to be consumers of a return attribution report from funds we are currently investing or planning to invest in. These reports can provide crucial insight into how a fund is generating its returns, and their attention to detail can give you insight into the diligence of their process.

The point of return attribution is not necessarily to document and audit every basis point of alpha. Rather, the process should be used to give you useful information about what is working, and perhaps even more importantly, what is not. It also helps evaluate what your opportunity set for performance is. We sometimes think outperformance comes from owning the best stocks in the best sectors. But you can also generate alpha from owning the best stocks in the worst sectors.

Many decisions are made when constructing your portfolios, but using levers and return attribution provides the shorthand for evaluating what happened and deciphering problems. Sometimes a strategy may be working, but the methods of expressing it are failing (right idea, wrong fund). Or sometimes the strategy itself is flawed. *But the response is different depending on where the fault lies!* Having a method **in place** to give you feedback is crucial to be able to respond appropriately. How often should this be monitored? There is certainly no answer for that. However, at the end of a year of underperformance, the question should not be "what happened?" but "what are we going to do?"

Any one trade has an impact on the portfolio returns and its deviation from your benchmark. You should have an idea of how far the trade can go against you, and what may precipitate a loss. This is basic risk management. The next step is keeping an awareness of how much the total portfolio may deviate from your benchmark. This is called Tracking Error.

Over any month the portfolio will rise and fall in degrees similar to the index. Some months the portfolio may outperform, some months it will underperform. A portfolio closely aligned to the benchmark will probably have returns that track closely to that benchmark. Tracking error is calculated as the standard deviation of the difference between the returns of the portfolio and its benchmark.

Tracking error can be derived from looking back at a portfolio's return relative to the index (ex-post tracking error). Why do we care about this? Shouldn't we be concerned only about relative returns – isn't alpha the only important thing? Tracking error can serve three purposes – 1. it offers an early warning signal that the portfolio may be vulnerable to underperformance, 2. it helps us target how much deviation from the index we can handle, and 3. it can also help guide the portfolio construction process.

An Early Warning Signal
If the portfolio over an extended period has similar returns to the benchmark we may assume its components are close enough without causing concern. However, if we were to see wild underperformance offset by outperformance each month, we should be concerned that something in the portfolio is causing unexpected volatility and should be examined.

A Target of Tolerated Deviation
We may have opinions and wish to express them, but at the end of the day, our job may not be to go our own way. We have a commitment to deliver returns according to our promise, as indicated by our benchmark. We may feel it would be inappropriate to underperform the index by more than 300bp, even if it forecloses an opportunity to outperform by more than that. We can look back on tracking error as a guardrail, and tighten our relative positioning if need be.

Portfolio Construction Guidance

As we build portfolios we may include input from tracking error to guide our allocations. Using Portfolio Visualizer (www.portfoliovisualizer.com) we can input tickers and use two different tools to guide us. The first is an optimization tool – we can create a list of tickers in the program and derive a minimum tracking error portfolio relative to a benchmark, or we can generate a maximum return portfolio subject to a target tracking error constraint. The latter approach would be influenced by the sectors with the highest return during the lookback period and should be used with caution. We can also use Portfolio Visualizer to backtest a portfolio with tickers and weights to find the tracking error it experienced. This provides a check on whether the portfolio you have conceived fits within your risk parameters.

Sophisticated modeling programs do exist that can present anticipated (ex-ante) tracking error, using comprehensive risk factor models. The model measures the portfolio's exposure to thousands of characteristics known to influence the volatility of security prices. Monte Carlo simulations can shock those factors, taking into account the volatility of those factors and the correlation between them, to determine how the returns of your portfolio could differ from that of the index. These programs help you manage your portfolio without forcing you to wait for a track of monthly reports to diagnose your risks. Blackrock 360 reports an ex-ante tracking error as "Estimated Active Risk".

This portfolio analyzed below has 174bp of ex-anti tracking error. That is, without looking at history but using a quantitative review of the risk sensitivities of the portfolio relative to the benchmark, the model calculates the returns can be expected to deviate 174bp from the benchmark's in any given year. But where does this risk come from? In this particular portfolio, 59bp is coming from GIC sector weights, and 77bp is from "Equity Style" generally meaning company size (small/mid/large cap) and valuation (value vs growth). 25bp comes from risk that is generally particular to individual companies and labeled "Idiosyncratic".

Risk Factor

Equity	1.47%
▪ Equity Market	0.04%
▪ Equity Country	0.07%
▪ Equity Sector	0.59%
▪ Equity Style	0.77%
Fixed Income	0.00%
▪ Rates	0.00%
▪ Spreads	0.00%
▪ Alternatives	0.00%
▪ FX	0.01%
▪ Idiosyncratic	0.25%
▪ Other	0.00%
Active Risk	**1.74%**

Source: Blackrock 360

It is possible the portfolio manager was deliberate in choosing these risks, both in **where** the risks were coming from but also the **magnitude** of potential impact. But it is also possible the manager built this portfolio with only a best guess as to how he was positioned relative to the benchmark. A vague preference for one sector can lead to inexact targeting of how much risk is truly taken.

With access to even more powerful tracking error models one can tease out very granular detail. In the example above we only know that the sector allocation causes a 59bp contribution to tracking error. But what if we wanted to know *which* sectors specifically? For example, as mentioned earlier energy companies are less correlated with the overall index, with big swings in performance relative to the overall market. Therefore, an overweight in that sector contributes a higher amount of tracking error than the same overweight in industrials, a sector more in line with market performance. With access to a more interactive model we can ask precise questions that may provide clarity on our risk allocation. Not only can we derive which sectors[53] contribute the most risk (sometimes called **component tracking error**), we can also determine the marginal risk impact of each sector, or even specific line items to small changes in their allocation (**marginal tracking error**). This is quite useful if for example you wanted to reduce tracking error and wanted to know which ETF you could add to or subtract from to accomplish that goal most efficiently. This information helps calibrate and define the risks you choose to take at a very granular level.

Using Tracking Error removes some of the inexact position sizing errors that can often occur. With this tool portfolio managers can be much more precise about which risks they are choosing to take, and how impactful those risks are. It is an elegance that elevates the art of portfolio management to a more purposeful practice.

---

[53] Using "sectors" generically to mean any portfolio position differentiation

Most financial advisors use outside managers to choose which specific stocks and bonds to buy. This can be through mutual funds, ETFs, or Separately Managed Accounts (SMAs). An advisor will use a manager obviously for security selection, but potentially for sector selection or tactical allocation as well. One should know in advance what role these managers are to play, as evaluation can only be accomplished in the context of what you want them to do.

There is a mystique about mutual fund managers and Wall Street types. They have an air of professionalism and knowledge, backed by deep research benches, and may carry an ego big enough to fill a room. Their demeanor can be intimidating. Yet for the most part the performance of most active managers is underwhelming. The probability of beating a large cap mandate is about 30%. The probability of beating it over a 10-year period is 11%. It is quite fair to question what they are doing and how they are doing it.

An advisor I know invested in a mid-cap event driven fund that had allocated over 30% in the materials sector, an overweight so massive it pulled up the entire portfolio's weighting to the sector. I asked the advisor if he liked the Materials sector that much. He said "it's not my decision, I'm just buying the fund and trusting them to take care of that stuff." That year the fund underperformed by 15%. Since you are owning the return, you should also own the process. It is your job to ask questions, and ask follow-up questions, and be satisfied with the answers. Like your own portfolios, you should know what they are trying to do, and whether it fits with your clients' needs.

If you think about your levers, analyzing funds can be more straightforward. For example, Beta is your most important lever. A global allocation or multi-strategy fund that has a baseline of 60% equity will never be appropriate for a client with a 90% equity allocation. That may seem clear. Now consider a value fund that keeps 20% in cash (ostensibly because the manager can't find enough cheap stocks to buy) and has a beta of 0.70. That fund is making a market-timing call, and hurting your clients' portfolio performance when the market rallies, while charging them fees for not investing. They are making beta bets that are not consistent with your mandate. Risk-adjusted returns are not sufficient if you require more risk!

You may find it helpful to categorize a fund to evaluate where it fits into your process and evaluate its results. Beyond the broad types (equity, money market, bond, etc) there is a differentiation of approach that bears elaborating, because their process can either complement yours, or be an execution of yours. Poorly chosen fund strategies can sabotage your work.

Concentrated Best Ideas Funds: These funds tend to have very few holdings and make no effort to look like a benchmark. Positions in these funds may have common characteristics (value or sector bias, for example) and their presence can skew your top-down positioning if owned in size because of the extreme concentration. These funds need to have demonstrated ability to generate alpha against your broad benchmark, because they are difficult to categorize and evaluate and their holdings can change dramatically. They introduce higher tracking error and volatility.

Single Focus Funds: These funds are more niche and easily comparable to a segment of the market. For example, a small cap growth sector fund can easily operate as an execution decision in your style box allocation to that sector. Evaluation is straightforward – did the fund outperform that sector, but importantly, if it did outperform, why? There is nuance even in niches, and you should be aware of potential sources of tracking error.

Focused Funds with Tactical Discretion: Some funds are given latitude to invest in a broad category but choose where to allocate within it. For example, the American Funds New Perspective fund invests in large cap growth stocks, but can vary the allocation between US stocks and International stocks, according to their view of best opportunities. In this sense, American Funds is pulling one of your levers for you. Tracking performance in this fund may be challenging given the fund straddles two concepts (allocation to large cap growth, and allocation to US vs Non-US) and has no "neutral", but given that growth is the dominant attribute, you would expect to measure performance vs other growth funds and metrics. Ideally, expert management can find the best stocks in the world within a small niche, producing research and execution that an advisor cannot recreate.

Index-Tracking Thematic Funds: There are many strategies that become popular, advertised as a method to beat broad indexes over the long term. For example, many dividend strategies are pegged to the performance of the S&P 500 Index. Though not direct mirrors, they often have sector allocations and attributes that minimize tracking error. Over time these funds expect to outperform but may deviate at times. They often confer some safety through lower volatility or better valuation. These strategies can go in and out of favor over the short term, but the managers expect alpha over long horizons. The best evaluation comparison may be other funds with similar styles or the broad index.

Near Passive: Many funds are either rules-based or specifically designed to minimize tracking error, but for small "tilts" towards one or more index attributes. This would also include factor and "Smart Beta" funds. Choosing these funds requires a desire for that tilt in the portfolio.

Global Allocation Funds and Balanced Funds: There are many hybrid funds that invest in both stocks and bonds, domestically and globally. In essence, they can be considered an outsourced Chief Investment Office. Some advisors use these funds as a dominant core holding for accounts. These funds make the tactical shifts for you, and if you believe in their process it may be appropriate for you. However, you still must know what their baseline is, because if it does not match your clients' baseline benchmark, it will not be a good fit for their portfolios. Another concern of holding bonds within a mutual fund multi-asset wrapper is it eliminates one of the advantages of holding bonds – liquidity at will. If you were to need to raise assets and not willing to sell stocks, you could not access the fixed income securities held in a balanced or global allocation fund independently of the stock positions. Owning bonds in a multi-asset mutual fund douses your volatility, without the benefit of liquidity, and can therefore be an inefficient way to hold your fixed income allocation. Also, evaluation of performance is difficult because of the multi-asset nature of the holdings and different baselines – a fund with a 40% bond neutral allocation will perform different from a fund with neutral allocation of 25%. Comparing performance requires you know where their neutral is. The evaluation work here is harder, even though the product is meant to make it easier for financial advisors to allocate a client and move on.

Go Anywhere Funds: These funds eschew the restraints of a benchmark and see the world as their opportunity set, like a San Diego surfer looking for the next big wave. They are bold in their allocation like concentrated best ideas funds, but not concerned with looking like, or being any particular type of fund. They also can be like global allocation funds, making tactical positioning for you. Without a baseline one will be highly challenged to evaluate performance. An advisor choosing a fund with such flexibility should be aware of its risks and impact on a total portfolio posture.

These are generally the categories available but there are certainly more that could be defined. And many funds may straddle more than one type. What is important is being able to recognize what you are looking at, so you can evaluate it according to the right context.

We have many options for using managers but should be conscious of the freedom we are giving them, and have some expectation of what you want them to do. If using a small-cap value fund, it need not outperform the S&P 500 Index, but how does it perform against a passive small cap value instrument? If using an aggressive and independent go anywhere fund, what is your standard of success? These questions should be asked before the investment is made, as it is meant to fill a role, or a void, within the overall portfolio.

EVALUATING MANAGERS – How are they doing it?

If investors knew in advance a mutual fund was going to be bad that fund wouldn't exist. Even storied fund managers have had career blighting moments. Returns are useful metrics if measured against the right context. I recently looked at a large cap growth mutual fund that posted big returns in 2020 that a client was excited about – except that it underperformed a passive large cap growth ETF. Returns are useful, but it's as important to know that the security's inclusion moves your portfolio where you need it to go.

There is no right metric or allocation for a fund to hit that declares it a winner. Sometimes a high P/E is indicative of aggressive revenue growth in a fund's constituent stocks, and a good sign. Sometimes a low P/E shows a savvy value investor. Results may just depend on the current market psyche, but that doesn't mean you shouldn't be aware of what you're getting into. Morningstar.com makes fund information accessible to everyone, democratizing the investment world somewhat.

Every fund has a detailed set of reports that describe the portfolio quantitatively. The style box can be viewed numerically, or graphically and compared with an index to see how broad the investment universe is for the fund.

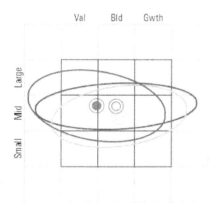

	Value	Blend	Growth
Large	7	24	0
Medium	14	33	4
Small	3	4	7

We can also see factor exposures and fundamental metrics:

Style	Yield	Momentum	Quality	Volatility	Liquidity	Size		Value & Growth Measures	Fund	Cat. Average	Index
Growth	High	High	High	High	High	Large		Price/Earnings	17.07	20.87	22.02
								Price/Book	2.96	2.26	2.30
								Price/Sales	1.74	1.53	1.47
								Price/Cash Flow	11.24	8.40	8.48
								Dividend Yield %	1.07	1.67	2.00
								Long-Term Earnings %	6.43	9.61	8.54
								Historical Earnings %	5.94	9.30	8.40
								Sales Growth %	2.02	5.50	6.04
								Cash-Flow Growth %	-0.26	6.97	5.62
Value	Low	Low	Low	Low	Low	Small		Book-Value Growth %	5.95	7.26	5.59

Source: Morningstar

We can build a dashboard of our levers to help us know where we are, and find new levers to adjust. There are some data points that are useful without being something we necessarily control as a lever. A fund's holding patterns are indicative of the management technique. Funds with only 20-40 holdings may be too concentrated, or maybe ideally targeted to fill in your gaps. Funds heavily concentrated in the top 10 holdings may be too vulnerable to idiosyncratic risk – that could introduce sensitivity into the overall portfolio. High turnover ratios may be a warning sign. If turnover is high but the fund underperforms, that could be a sign of a failing strategy. Conversely, a fund that targets momentum stocks may be expected to rotate to the stocks that are currently successful. And of course high fees and poor performance against its niche are red flags.

There are no rules for this, and even recent success may not be enough to qualify or disqualify a fund (though it's certainly a consideration). What matters in fund evaluation is whether what it did makes sense. If a fund succeeded, you must understand what it did right and whether it can be replicated. If a fund underperformed, you must understand the process and decide if it has merit in the right environment.

A major wirehouse brokerage offered their clients a rules-based portfolio that was reconstituted annually based on parameters that identified high quality, high dividend stocks. The portfolio rules were unconstrained by sector allocation matching any index and the number of included stocks was very small, so tracking error was significant. But many financial advisers used this model because the long term returns were quite good. Another characteristic of this portfolio was it excluded financial stocks. Any lookback period that included the 2008 financial crisis (when financial stocks were devastated) would show substantial outperformance, but the exclusion of Financials was not a decision based on valuation or tactical foresight. Rather, it was an artifact of the portfolio rules. Many financial advisors invested in this strategy without understanding it, and experienced years of sometimes dramatic underperformance.

The due diligence process is often summarized as a review of the 5 P's: People, Philosophy, Process, Portfolios, Performance, and Price. We must understand and trust the managers' professionalism and experience. We have to believe their philosophy for investing has merit, and they have a process to turn their worldview into an efficient invested portfolio that can be managed and adapted to new information. We examine whether the resultant portfolio reflects what the manager expressed as their intention, and whether it conforms with our own expectations and needs. Then we evaluate whether the manager delivers performance appropriate for the risks and allocation. Of course it's not simple, but having a disciplined process in our own due diligence is part of the value we bring to clients.

Fund evaluation is an ongoing process – even after you have invested, every moment you keep it you are reaffirming its role in your clients' portfolios. Over time, these funds reallocate. Some are winners, some are suffering. You may adjust your levers or you may feel a fund does not express an attribute as much as you thought it would, or as much as it had in the past. Or a fund has sensitivities you never realized. Surveillance should never end.

CONSEQUENCES OF AN INFORMATION DEFICIT

To summarize: A thoughtful portfolio construction process, accompanied by ongoing tracking and periodic evaluation, is the best way to keep control.

Mike Tyson famously said "everyone has a plan until they get punched in the mouth." This can easily apply to investing as well as boxing. When we create portfolios, we certainly expect them to do well. There must be some thesis, some reason why these benchmark deviations are better than a passive approach. With some bravado some portfolio managers count their alpha when they put the trade on. And when things go badly it's hard for them to recalibrate. That is why when we build a portfolio, we have also built a process – we hope to have created a winning concept, but also a capacity to *learn!*

Without a process and risk control, there is likely to be a moment when you've underperformed by a significant amount and questions have to be asked. Was it a specific fund? An allocation? You bought all these funds that had superior risk adjusted returns and they all trailed the index. How did that happen?

Without the language and analytics for portfolio management, it can feel like a very dark place with too many questions.

- What went wrong?
- Which fund/stocks/assets caused it?
- What were my bets?
- How big were my bets?
- What has to change?
- How much has to change?
- Is it too late?
- Will it recover?

Our instincts are to correct, but we may lack the clarity (both informationally and emotionally) to adjust appropriately.

It would be better to have the clarity to ask these questions:

- Which levers were I pulling?

146

- How big were those trades?
- How volatile were those trades?
- Were they more volatile than I expected?
- Did my funds underperform their mandate?
- Did I underperform in an unexplainable way, indicating unexpected exposures?
- Was my tracking error larger than expected?
- Is there a better target allocation?

These questions shift the nature of the inquiry towards an evaluation of portfolio assumptions against realized experience. We can see whether our portfolio responded the way we thought it should, and if it didn't, we can correct towards our targeted goals clinically (though regretfully). If it responded exactly as expected then we can revisit the levers we were using, and reevaluate our tolerance for risk (as defined by tracking error).

At the same time, unexpected outperformance is just as much a symptom of risk. We might be inclined to clap our hand and move on after a good year, but if outperformance cannot be explained there is a blind spot in your portfolio allocation that can hurt you later. The goal of careful portfolio construction is to choose the risks we want to take. *Randomness in portfolio returns is often the unexamined repercussions of a choice.* For example, an Equal Weighted S&P 500 ETF may be chosen for its alpha potential, but you are also choosing a bias towards mid-cap stocks over large cap stocks (compared to a market weighted index) and also weighting sectors by the number of stocks in each sector regardless of their size. The impact on your levers occurs regardless of your intention.

Future returns are always an unknown, but the problem is compounded when the present is as dark. Severe market moves seem like they require a response, an adjustment. But we can make changes precipitously if not grounded in facts. Over a long horizon, we may not be wrong even if it feels very bad in the moment. Or, we can be so overwhelmed by sudden negative feedback that our ability to navigate is impaired. How we manage information over the entire course can mitigate the risk of making quick decisions on imperfect information.

If you understand the portfolio as a collection of compensated risks, it is easier to put in context what you are trying to do, how you are expressing your views, and whether the portfolio is responding the way you'd expect it should. The language of portfolio management can be arcane, but its specificity allows for more control. The process is important not because it gives you the answers, but because it gives you the questions.

PART SIX: MANAGING MONEY
DEVELOPING A WORLD VIEW

The narrative thus far has dealt with the mechanics and theory of investing and hasn't dealt with the art. Things like investment tracking and establishing a benchmark and managing your levers are *must do* aspects of portfolio management. They are intellectually interesting questions and fun in the sense that there are no wrong answers as long as they are exploratory. Moreover, if you were passive versus your benchmark there'd be nothing left to do.

The rest is art. Your portfolio may be more Kandinsky with geometric orderliness to it, or more inspired with chaotic precision like a Jackson Pollack. I would not criticize anyone's style as long as they understood what they were *trying* to do. Some advisors become prisoner of their line items, bought for a forgotten reason at a moment when it seemed to look good. **Without a good reason to buy an asset, they lack a good reason to sell it.** The portfolio's levers are like lumpy old play doh, insensitive and hard to wield.

That's why focus should be given to the levers of your portfolios. Pulling them is functionally easy. Once you have isolated the metrics you want to follow and have a method for viewing potential investments as an instrument for moving your levers, placing a buy order is simple. We must be careful, however, to realize that pulling levers should be done judiciously. Using a lever is **expressing a view**. *Why do you have that view?*

I was on a conference call with a Wall Street strategist who had just finished a presentation deck on his outlook for the US economy. A financial advisor came over the line and said "great presentation but what do I *do* with this." An interesting question, philosophically. Many investors build their model portfolio and leave it unchanged barring significant world events. Others would listen to the daily pulse and make changes as seems fit. The answer to the advisor's question depends on your view of your fiduciary duty. If you are constructing an all-weather portfolio, infrequent small-nudges may be the extent of your activity. Conversely if you have a more dynamic approach then you may have more use for high frequency data and market reviews. Your consumption and response to information should be predicated on how and which levers you control. Once

149

your levers are defined, new information can be incorporated naturally into the portfolio management process.

The first caution to think about is as follows: If you've designed the benchmark to be appropriate, why should your client portfolios diverge from it? What reasons could justify changes? There may be a preference for a simple benchmark when your long-term views are more granular and require a permanent divergence. For other temporary adjustments, what is driving the decision?

Any approach is valid as long as you have some framework. Advisors and portfolio managers can make their decisions based on relative value compared to historical relationships. P/E ratios of sectors relative to where they have been historically, or divergence in value/growth performance are examples. Analysts can follow the business cycle and note where the economy is with respect to growth and retraction. Bottom-up managers can note the balance sheet fundamentals of industrial sectors and allocate to the best prospects. Relying on gut instincts and winging it are not good strategies for managing portfolios.

The information you collect and use as a reference helps develop your worldview. Much thought should be spent thinking about investment process. What is your pitch that explains how you see the investment environment right now? Given that pitch, how would you structure a portfolio? What are the levers you would pull to express that view? Which funds or stocks are you using to execute that? You should endeavor to have a straightforward train of thought that gets you from an outlook on the world or markets, to a portfolio that says the same thing. It may help to write it down, and look at it every day. Because there will be a day when you see what you wrote, and disagree. And the portfolio must change.

If your active bets are directly linked to the levers you want to pull, unwinding them is easy. Getting to neutral is easy, but only if you have connected the dots all the way from outlook to execution.

Oscar Wilde described a cynic as one who knows the price of everything and the value of nothing. Indeed, when we become fixated on asset prices and oblivious to the value, we indulge in a gamesmanship approach to investing. Price may be helpful in evaluating investments, but we cannot ignore value. If we are cognizant of value we would not be deterred by "record high prices" if the fundamentals are supportive. Conversely, after a market correction we still may not be persuaded by calls that "stocks are cheap!" if earnings are significantly depressed.

Put another way, Benjamin Graham wrote "…most investment advisors take their opinions and measures of stock values from stock prices. In the stock market, value standards do not determine prices; prices determines value standards."

We use the terms overvalued and undervalued, or rich and cheap, to describe a market's valuation. These terms are useful descriptors, but it is important to elaborate what they imply. An overvalued market does not mean an investor **will** lose money, it means an investor is likely to earn a lower return than expected based on historical experience. An undervalued market implies a higher than typical return. Calling back to the lessons from the efficient frontier, if expected return for one asset is now lower relative to its volatility, portfolio adjustments should perhaps be made if there are alternative assets that offer a better risk/return tradeoff for the portfolio. When we recall the initial description of a portfolio as a collection of compensated risks, it reminds us to evaluate whether we are compensated enough for the risk we are taking.

When we are investing in multi-asset portfolios we do have options for how we embrace risk. When stocks are "rich", repositioning to less overvalued asset classes such as real estate or private credit may protect the portfolio without sacrificing too much expected return, and maintaining the return target that will deliver the results indicated in the financial plan.

That said, there is a distance from making an evaluation that a particular market is overpriced, and the practical implications of trading in and out of risk. Too often we view our options as "risk on / risk off" which is a simple but sometimes naïve approach. As discussed before, the most impactful lever to pull is Beta; the decision to be invested in the market or not.[54] It may also be the easiest lever to manipulate because you can sell any market asset and you effectively reduce beta. It is also cheap - with index funds and ETFs competing to reduce fees to nearly nothing, Beta is nearly free to own and trade. We are also constantly encouraged to be thinking about Beta with pundits and analysts inundating the airwaves with commentary. "Stocks have never been this cheap, according to THIS metric!" "The rally is over, is a bear market coming!?" The breathless delivery almost makes it seem trivial, and yet it can propel you to make one of your biggest mistakes.

Unfortunately the attempt to value the market can lead to hyperbolic declarations of extremes. The pessimists can seem very persuasive and the optimists can be so enthusiastic. Unfortunately, there are no absolute rules that always work. (If there was a rule the markets would not be efficient!) The market can be very irrational, and insisting on everything making immediate sense means you can lose out on significant upside.

Going up is a natural direction for the market, because stocks are valued with an expectation of a return on investment. Market pessimists have a larger burden to prove - that either the valuation is too high (the discount rate too low) or *long term* market earnings expectations will not be realized. Market optimists need only expect that the future's earnings forecast will become today's retained earnings and productive assets. This is not to say that stocks always go up, they assuredly go down too, and can fall precipitously as assumptions change. It is only over long periods of time that stocks are very likely to generate returns.

You always need to understand **what are your investment alternatives?** When the US 10-year Treasury Note is offering 7% yield, the stock market must offer a substantially higher expected return to compete with a product with virtually no default risk. You need a risk premium, the extra return over riskless investments, to justify volatility. On the other hand, when the 10-year Treasury Note is only 1%, the required return on stocks can be much lower. For example, instead of using a 10% required return (discount rate) on stocks, analysis may begin using 7%. In your Excel spreadsheet you'd see an immediate jump in a stock's value.

---

[54] As a reminder, beta can be very nuanced. Though in general we are talking about the "stock market", or any market, we can also be speaking about precisely how much market exposure relative to a specific index we are targeting.

In the market you may see a transition to much higher prices over a short time. Pessimists would say it's an irrational rally. If interest rates did fall to 1% or lower it would be in the context of an economy in duress (and low inflation), and earnings would likely be depressed. But mathematically a market rally would make sense, to the extent that investors did not have any other investment choices that could produce yield. When interest rates rise, the opposite occurs.

There are plenty of metrics that investors use to gauge stock market valuation, here are just a few approaches:

- Price / Earnings ratios (forward, trailing, cyclically adjusted)
- Price / Cash Flow
- Market capitalization vs Gross National Product
- Dividend Yield minus US 10-Year Treasury
- Earnings Yield (inverse of P/E ratio) minus Corporate Bond Yield
- Arbitrary pain rules (example P/E + Inflation > 20 is expensive)

All of these can be tracked, and they should be tracked, but making a call on market direction is an explicit judgement that the market is overvalued and wrong, and you are right. The market **value** can be dramatically wrong, but sometimes it's just a little bit wrong, and it can stay that way for a very long time, during which the natural tendency of companies to increase profits can catch up underneath it. The earnings may increase faster than the price, compressing P/E ratios. Instead of seeing a big collapse, you may see a period of low returns, while you were sitting out.

We tend to see market timing as a beta on / beta off decision. Dry powder on the side. But we do have more marginal choices. We can overweight utility or high dividend stocks with lower Beta. We can invest in foreign markets with more attractive valuation. Since the Beta decision is so impactful, we should definitely do the math beforehand and ask ourselves – how much underperformance can I stand, and therefore how much Beta can I afford to sell.

When trying to out-guess the market always be aware of what you think the market doesn't know and why you are right. Be sure to track the evidence of your assumption. If you are sure earnings will disappoint, you should track leading indicators and bellweather stocks for direction, and a time frame to admit the market may have been less wrong than you.

I want to say there is no *wrong* way to invest because these pages are not about judgement, just education, and we can all have different good faith perspectives. With that said, I've seen many portfolios built by professionals that have damaged their clients' financial position, either through unexpected risk in short options strategies, excess exposure to illiquid instruments, or (less damning) big underweights to favored sectors. On the other hand, some professional investors end their portfolio management responsibilities after picking funds from a list based on recent performance. We may all have different legitimate investing approaches, but being uneducated or lackadaisical is not a style.

Many investors' personality comes through in the way they invest. Some traits help you towards success, others may be beneficial but need to be contained. Being impulsive may keep you ahead of the curve and able to react to changes you see. Whether you are looking at new technologies or able to spot consumer trends first, anyone who has the vision can be a tremendously successful portfolio manager. However, impulsiveness is reckless if it means being brash and indifferent to financials and the economics of an idea. On the other hand, caution, diligence, and patience are fine attributes – unless it leads to sclerotic decision making. A portfolio manager doesn't have to be any one type of person, but will perform best if he knows the weaknesses of his best attributes.

As you develop as a portfolio manager, you will hopefully incorporate a process from portfolio construction framework, to investment decision, to portfolio review. What is important though is that your process for choosing investments does not become a bias. I spoke to a mutual fund portfolio manager who ran an event-driven mid cap growth strategy – the approach was to look for companies that might have imminent corporate events such as a restructuring, buyout, or ownership changes that would unleash value. They were looking for a tangible and measurable benefit that could occur, where the value of a company presently was less than the sum of its potential parts. This approach is sensible, but the fund was significantly overweight in industrials and materials stocks, because the rigor of their process excluded companies they couldn't value in that way. Though the process may have been sound, the drift from the market portfolio introduced a bias. A financial advisor must be aware of the bias in an investment (or his own process), because as allocation increases the bias will dominate returns.

It is important to understand that the way you see the world can inform you, or blind you. An advisor who is enamored with high dividend payment stocks runs the risk of missing fast growing companies not yet paying out earnings, and concentrating investment in specific sectors. Advisors who concentrate in fast growing companies run the risk of overpaying, and defy the history which has indicated that Value stocks tend to outperform.

As you build portfolios, it is understandable to have a perspective on investing. Part of the process should be to evaluate the process. What is the view you are taking? What is the opposite of that view, and can you argue it is wrong? How do you monitor the legitimacy of your thesis over time?

As an advisor, you are best positioned to care for your clients' financial health, and you should feel free to invest as you see appropriate and prudent. But it is important for you, as a manager, to understand what kind of investor you are. What are your personality traits that are helpful? What may be the drawbacks of your method? Self-awareness may help you spot future problems.

As discussed before, strategic investment decisions that are intended to be long-term or permanent are best declared in your choice of benchmark. If you have a permanent preference for US domiciled companies or an underweight to Large Cap stocks, at the outset of your client relationship you should indicate the metrics for which you want to be held accountable.

That said, there are three good reasons to keep it simple. First, it's simple. Explaining to clients that you use four different indexes to represent your strategy may actually be a lot of explaining that is too granular for some clients and a simpler benchmark is more readily explained. Second, it may be a long term allocation that is not necessarily a permanent one, and changing benchmarks is a lot harder to explain than changing investments. And finally, some investment tilts are not easily captured in a benchmark – for example, a long term decision to overweight ESG (Environment, Social, and Governance) factors. You may not have an absolute dedication to a theme but choose to own certain funds and push the allocation in a desired direction. That would be a strategic view that could not be readily defined in a benchmark.

Strategic trades are not predicated on the whims of the random walk, but on secular changes in the world around us. Whereas a tactical trade may be as quick as turning on the light, strategic trades are more like the coming of the dawn. Strategic investing is a patient game that need not be watched every day, though of course the impact should be acknowledged and tracked. The investors who bet against the mortgage market during the financial crisis were convinced of their trade. They did not need daily fluctuations to know the bust was coming, even though it was a painful wait. In the same way, strategic trades should have a view supported by research and investigation. A good trade is probably not obvious, it only seems that way after the fact.

Tactical trades are meant to be short term views. They are driven by a belief in temporary changes in relative value – be it a market timing trade or a belief that one sector is undervalued relative to another. The important distinction is that these trades are put on with a view that something will happen, and the reason for the trade will disappear. Because of that, the investor must be vigilant, tracking the trade's success, evaluating its ongoing prospects, and deciding how to react when it seems to be progressively wrong.

Through inactivity or inattention, tactical trades can become strategic trades. This usually happens when you are wrong.[55] This is a very dangerous place to be as you've already lost alpha for a client on a bad idea. You have three choices: close the trade, increase the trade because if you thought it was good before it must be twice as good now, or do nothing. If it goes back to where your put the trade on, you lose nothing, gain nothing. But if it keeps going badly at some point it's a deadly weight on your returns. And yet doing nothing feels easier than admitting defeat, and it lingers as you become more adamant that you will eventually be right. At some point "eventually" becomes a strategic belief.

Tactical trades require vigilance, but also a mental stop loss that you are comfortable with in advance will help. It removes the emotion and minimizes loss. One hopes that a single loss would be offset by gains on other trades, and on-net your decisions bring value to clients. One would also hope that if your decisions are not generating alpha you are aware of the fact. Your ongoing attribution work and tracking should tell you what you are good at, and you would be wise to concentrate on those activities.

Understanding the difference between tactical and strategic trades will help you manage your risk, and manage communication with your clients. Furthermore, you help yourself understand what you are trying to do and prepare yourself for when it seems to go wrong. You should not expect to be wrong, but it is helpful to know how you will respond when you are.

---

[55] Wrong in that the trade has led to a current loss of alpha – it may still be fundamentally correct, and that is the difficulty.

Moving a portfolio away from its benchmark is an active bet. Hopefully every decision is carefully thought out and defensible, and you understand the **cumulative** tracking error you have welcomed into the portfolio. When everything goes right, or enough goes right, you can be lulled into complacency and not keep your eye on the total **risk** you are taking. In this context, we are using 'risk' as another word for *underperformance.*

What becomes apparent when you are on the losing side of a trade is your capacity to make new trades can feel closed off. You should allow yourself a certain amount of potential deviation. You should be able to state your tolerance and know what your potential for exceeding that is. With a sophisticated tracking error model you can track your risk with every trade you make. A back of the envelope method of looking at historical trade deviations may be the best you have, but better than nothing. Having a framework to understand your risk (of underperformance) helps you control your impulses, and avoid getting over your skis in a bad situation.

Unfortunately, when you are on the wrong side of a trade that is big enough to impact portfolio returns, you find that your risk budget is eaten up. If you were not willing to lose more than 2% vs the benchmark, and you find yourself there, your ability to "trade out of it" should be curtailed. You feel you cannot put on new trades until the old trades work out, and every new trade introduces more risk.

A portfolio manager is in a difficult position when they are behind. Do more of what didn't work, or respect the boundaries of a risk budget and wait. Both are mentally distressing. Trading defensively, trying to correct mistake in order to stop losses distracts you, preventing clear headed thinking about good trades you could otherwise make. Flailing wildly is no good either.

Proactive trading is mentally healthier – try to be in a position of trading on offense. Being on offense means you see opportunities and can take advantage of them. You have superior real time information that you feel the market has not digested, you are not following popular trades, and you can defend the trade concept. As you become more active, always keep in mind the tracking error you are incurring on each trade – know how much you can handle and how much risk you already have. Keep more volatile trades smaller.[56] Be aware of how much of your risk budget is already eaten up.

In a simpler world we could just choose to be ahead, but the market doesn't work that way. As financial advisors and portfolio managers our job is to minimize the risk we will be at a trading disadvantage. Being boxed in on bad trades can feel debilitating. Part of good management is controlling your enthusiasm and your confidence, and confronting the possibility you could be not just wrong, but very wrong. Investing during dire times can be a grind, like a game of chess after losing a queen and two rooks. But you don't get to give up and start with a new board. Take deep breaths, and figure out what you can still do, and what you **should** do.

---

[56] As noted earlier, a "smaller" trade is not necessarily the one with fewer dollars invested, but the one with a larger potential alpha impact because of its volatility relative to the benchmark.

PLAN FOR OPPORTUNITIES

I've seen many client portfolios where an advisor leaves cash on the side for "dry powder". It's a very curious thing, mostly because I've seen market corrections occur and somehow that cash on the side never manages to be deployed into the portfolio. Generally those opportunities are the scariest moments to invest. That cash remains a permanent drag on performance that the client is paying good money for you to manage and invest. Even with the best intentions, what generally happens is when big moves happen we are always unprepared for it. Dry powder is only good if you can use it.

Opportunities come quickly. Dislocations occur when something surprising happens, or when bad news begins to look really, really bad. When England voted to break from the European Union (Brexit) there was an immediate global reaction and alarm, that reversed promptly. When the COVID-19 pandemic fears first hit, the broader equity market fell nearly 40%, even for companies that would likely benefit from a transition to online and cloud revenue. But recoveries happen quickly as well. When scary things happen our first inclination is to hide. But in the market, scary things may be our best friends. There are far more opportunities during dislocations than there are in "normal times".

When the market is in crisis, you may have a short amount of time to research your options and execute. It is during these times that managing your levers is the most crucial. How do you know where valuation is by sector? How do you know which sectors are hardest hit? How do you know what is cheapest to historical norms? Developing the research during the crisis may be too late. The information you need to make decisions should always be ready and at your grasp. During the Covid selloff in 2020, the S&P 500 Index was in a deep spiral for just a month before beginning to recover. The stock price of the giant internet retailer Amazon, a now obvious winner of the economic rebalancing, began its recovery in just 24 calendar days.

As an ongoing process, even when it's boring and the information is not tradable, you should have control of your data and processes. If every week you review the information that drives your levers, nod your head and say "uh huh", you are ensuring the system works. There are no blown spreadsheet links, the formulas still work, data integrity is maintained. Because one day, there will be a moment when those efficient markets are acting with paranoia, and there will be a trade that looks so good, it almost shouldn't exist.

Don't let dry powder sit there for years. Don't wait for dire situations to spur you to have a research process. Assume that you will have opportunities to make critical decisions and build a platform for rigorous due diligence. Your success during crises will be far greater than the singles and doubles you may hit in "normal" times. There's no reason to waste the moment thinking about what you need to know.

Investment management aspires to be a science, though it falls short because in science good experiments can be replicated. With investments, it is very hard to recreate an experience exactly, and even when an event looks like something from the past, it still manages to evolve differently. Furthermore, the smartest scientists are by definition the leaders in their field, but it sometimes seems the smartest investors lose the most money. Due to this lack of clarity about what is the "right" process, there are thousands of books on the topic, including this one – though I argue this work is about how to *think* about the investment decisions you make, not how to make them.

Your investment style may push you into either bottom-up, or top-down management. Top-down analysis looks at the portfolio as a cohesive whole, and choices retain a macro narrative. The individual securities are less important than the portfolio's overall posture. This book emphasizes a top-down approach, not because it is easier or better, but because your choices are clearly defined and since idiosyncratic risks are assumed to be diversified away, we can concentrate on fewer variables. Controlling your levers is easier, since you have defined the portfolio against them and changing them does not require adjusting a dedicated, well-researched individual position.

Bottom-up analysis adherents may scoff at that approach. They may say: "At the end of the day, you are buying (mostly) stocks and bonds, and you should be intimately knowledgeable about every investment decision. Hugging an index or passive management is irresponsible because you are abdicating your duty to evaluate investment ideas. Indeed, indices themselves are arbitrary barometers of success. Buying good companies is the role of an investment manager." A bottom-up manager may have fewer positions that they have high confidence in.

There is nothing wrong with that view and I have tremendous sympathy for the view that more research is better than less, but with this caveat: just because you do not look at your risk a certain way, it doesn't mean you don't have it. The market does not care how you look at your portfolio, and if your methodology leads to an underinvestment in a sector or attribute that has been doing very well, you should know. Eventually it will be clear.

Of course these are absolutes, and top-down investors can be very concerned about their individual positions, and bottom-up investors are certainly aware of their overall portfolio positioning. Rather, you need to be aware of your preferred approach, and aware of any biases that may become part of it. As the investment advisor, you have to be comfortable with the approach and be able to explain its virtues and flaws to your clients.

Those who have taken the Series 7 exam are familiar with the questions asked to evaluate your knowledge of Put options. "A client wants to **hedge** his portfolio, which instrument would you suggest." For new entrants into the financial world it may be a misleading introduction to an important topic. The use of the word hedge is thrown around carelessly.

When you actually hedge you are neutralizing risk. A bond trader who buys a corporate bond may sell same duration Treasury bonds to eliminate interest rate risk. An options trader who sells a call option may buy stock in the underlying company. But a financial advisor who buys index puts to reduce his market beta is not reducing his risk **with respect to his mandate.** *The financial advisor's long term neutral position is his pre-determined allocation to stocks that he and his client agreed was appropriate.*

Any deviation from that is not reducing risk, it is increasing risk of deviation from that target. One may capture higher returns if the market falls, or lost returns if markets rise. What is crucial to understand is that this trade is a *market timing* trade, not a hedging trade. Calling it a hedge denatures what you are accomplishing, and attempts to present an active trade as a risk reduction effort.

I learned the nuance of this concept when I managed an international bond portfolio with no US dollar exposure. Sensing that the Euro was overvalued, I "hedged" some of my currency exposure by selling it in the forward market, thinking I was reducing the portfolio's currency risk. The Euro promptly appreciated, leaving me with losses and my portfolio underperformed versus the benchmark. What occurred to me later was my perception was all wrong. Nobody would care that I "reduced risk" since the fund's mandate accepted the currency positions. My trading was strictly a market timing bet with no risk mitigation benefits, from the perspective of my client, and my loss had no silver lining.

A true hedge will reduce unwanted exposure that would remain as long as the overall position or trade is active. For example, a bond trader would hedge his interest rate sensitivity whenever he was keeping a bond in his inventory. It would be a permanent, systematic process that would live as long as he owned that inventory position. Another example could be a portfolio sensitivity that creeps in alongside an active bet. For example, if a portfolio manager chooses to overweight Financial stocks, he may be susceptible to underperformance if interest rates decline, as banks earn more money when interest rates are higher. He may hedge that risk by including Real Estate Investment Trusts (REITs) that may outperform when interest rates go down. An investor who has an overweight to Value stocks may find that his exposure to the Momentum factor was reduced, and he could hedge this by adding Momentum ETFs to restore his balance. Thinking more broadly, investors may use their portfolio to hedge other risks in their life. An owner of a trucking company may overweight the Energy sector if his corporate profits are reduced when oil prices rise. Or airlines may hedge the price of oil so they could have more clarity on their business costs.

Hedges are used to reduce risks that occur as a byproduct, and may be sustained as long as the risk persists. If you are turning the hedge on and off, or actively seeking the risk as part of normal operations, then thinking of it as a hedge is inappropriate. The concern is that a trade conceived as a hedge leads to losses, and leads you to take more risk to recover. Understanding a trade's purpose helps control the situation and prevents it from getting out of hand. Just remember that a "hedge" that takes a client off his path is never a hedge.

I listened to a conference recently about evaluating an investment strategy and the speaker said it takes ten years, or through an entire market cycle, to evaluate a strategy. He was speaking academically, where you could replicate a specific factor approach that had been validated by historical data. I've heard admonishments from mutual fund managers arguing the same, that quarterly performance means nothing, only long term results are relevant for evaluation. There is some legitimacy to this because over short periods there can indeed be divergences between benchmark and portfolio returns that are evened out or reversed over time.

There are equally valid counterarguments to only taking the long view. The first is simple: your capacity for underperformance is limited to your clients' tolerance for it. It would indeed be wonderful if you had ten years to get it right but that probably will not happen. Underperformance will need to be explained.

Even if your clients gave you a decade to deliver benchmark beating returns, this is still problematic. From a practical standpoint, you, as the manager, need information, and even short-term underperformance is feedback. If you are not paying attention to returns you do not know when you've made mistakes. Even worse, you do not learn from them.

Most financial advisors are not "born investors." While most books on the subject deal with picking stocks and finding alpha, you are still forced to grope your way through the muddy, mental slog that is managing portfolios. Making mistakes is inevitable, and scalding. Losing money is memorable, and if you can catalogue the behaviors that led to problems, or the financial fundamentals you missed, you are less likely to repeat them. If you have not understood your mistakes, you cannot prevent them from happening again.

Another weakness of ignoring short-term results is missing bad situations that continue to get worse. Some events are slow motion disasters that may be obvious to those paying attention. Efficient markets would suggest there is nothing you can do, but if you were making active bets then you are probably not convinced by that theory. That said, some situations devolve with plenty of time to adjust. Some investors in General Electric stock saw the deteriorating fundamentals and weakness in the dividend and reduced their position. Others were enamored with the high dividend yield and stayed on board as the stock fell from $30 per share to $12 when it drastically cut its payout. Soon after it was trading at less than $7. After the collapse I checked with three different fund managers that specialized in high dividend stocks for their sale price: one sold just over $32, one at $28, and one around $10. Maybe you wouldn't have made any changes, but being *aware* gives you the choice of responding.

Not all situations of course require course correction. Tesla has had a volatile track and I knew investors who were actively shorting it. Those who ignored the downtrend and held on have been handsomely rewarded. I am not here suggesting that a sinking stock requires a quick sale. I am saying positions that are affecting your performance should be understood, and if the investment thesis has changed then action may be required. It could also indicate a larger position is appropriate!

If you have positions that deviate from your benchmark and can lead to underperformance, you are taking active bets. Investing requires time and attention – if you have neither, client portfolios should look like their benchmark. Active positioning assumes an ability to attend to short term results. We may want to restrain a tendency to over react, but looking far into the horizon and expecting your active portfolios to keep to the path may be too optimistic.

Good investing is more clearly defined by what it is "not". Chasing winners, being swayed by marketing and expensed dinners, promoting products that pay high commissions – these are all dangerous roads because the realized portfolio can be an ugly mass of independent ideas that don't gel into a single purposeful thesis. What belongs and what doesn't? What does the advisor believe about the markets? A good portfolio should not need an explanation. It should be able to speak for itself without guidance.

I spoke to a financial advisor who employed different models for most of his clients' accounts. Fifty different mutual funds were found among them, some only appearing once. I asked why he used one, and he shrugged and said "it looked good at the time." A good investor should know what he is trying to do, understand why every piece fits and makes sense. Portfolio managers can have an investment aesthetic, a look or feel that is consistent. Developing an aesthetic helps you articulate what you are trying to do.

Your investment choices are like colors in a palette. Dividend yield, high growth, momentum, sector biases, focus funds, factor tilts – everything is like a color you can paint on the portfolio. Bold concentrations are like a heavy brush. Opposing trades – overweight momentum and defensive stocks for example – can create a balance. Sometimes you can be a reproduction, just slightly off from the familiar strokes of an index. Sometimes your views are defiantly drawn. At all times your vision should be presented as a sensible narrative.

The randomness of the markets makes it hard to distinguish the lucky from the good. I read a due diligence report on a mutual fund that warned because the process was deemed deficient, the returns would likely be lower – a difficult to prove conclusion. Even the least prepared can outperform, and the most diligent may suffer. High returns are not the automatic reward for the most prepared. Those that do the work simply have the confidence that they have made as few mistakes as they could.

Every strategy will have good years and bad. What matters is that you understand your strategy and do the best work you can, because conviction isn't enough. Designing your portfolios that express your views, your outlook, and your fundamental beliefs will keep you from feeling vertigo when things don't go your way. Controlling your levers and portfolio attributes won't automatically dig yourself out of a mess, but it will show you where to dig.

Your aesthetic – the levers you like to control, how aggressively you set them, the type of funds you invest in – helps you manage yourself. Understand what it is you do and how it's different from other managers. Do you have a philosophy that guides you? What information do you absorb? What makes you trade? As an investor, what are the core beliefs you stand on?

Our images of professional investors can look like Gordon Gecko from the movie "Wall Street" extolling the virtues of greed, or Tom Wolfe's confident "Masters of the Universe" description of bond traders moving millions of dollars around without blinking. Or the cool young rogues who lose billions then frantically try to cover their mistakes.

The truth is that investing is a grind, a marathon that hopefully never ends because your clients keep trusting you. The investing profession tends to attract "alpha" types who think they know better than the market. Indeed, having attitude is a good way to start if it gives you the energy to do the research, do the due diligence, and truly understand your market, but one needs to have fortitude to keep going when you've been wrong, and to keep finding solutions and keep digging for ideas even when you're most recent ones went bad.

There is academic literature on the mental mistakes that can make us bad investors called Behavioral Finance.   This subset of finance studies how psychology influences our rational decision making. The subconscious bias we bring to our trading activity can be as pernicious as not paying attention to a losing trade, and being aware of our tendencies helps us control them.

A couple of these investor ticks are worth reviewing briefly. **Anchoring** is when an investor uses recent experience or information to create an expectation of value or return.   Information is helpful in decision making, but as it ages its relevance decreases. When GE fell from 30 to 20, many thought it was cheap because it used to be 30. That did not stop it from falling further. While the price obviously fell, *new* information was revealed about deep structural problems within the company. In a vacuum, if price was your only piece of information, then indeed, GE did look cheap at 20. History is a wonderful guide, but context matters.   The recent explosive returns of the FANG stocks present similar Anchoring conundrums. Will they *always* have outsized returns? Certainly not. But recent performance creates a misleading case that it will go on forever.

One common feature of investors is they don't like to realize losses – it implies they made a mistake. One emotional power at the disposal of investors is choosing when to acknowledge that mistake. It has been noticed in financial market research that investors tend to hold on to their losing positions far longer than their winning ones. This is known as a **Disposition Bias.** The refusal to accept mistakes prevents us from allocating towards more rewarding investments.

I've heard many times someone say "it's not a loss until you sell." This must be considered in context – where could you have invested instead of this position? Every day you have a portfolio that you choose to keep, you get to decide which positions to hold and which to sell. If the price of an asset falls, portfolio value falls and you suffer a loss. It may recover, or it may not, and you must re-evaluate whether your research was faulty, or if the asset is even cheaper now and more attractive. Though selling feels like the end, that you've committed to the concept that you were wrong, in truth every day you keep it is a re-commitment that you still like it. If the valuation metrics you use to buy an asset still indicate it has value, it should be kept! Should it no longer look attractive we should not move the goal post to accommodate a wounded ego.

The objectiveness of how we use information can also lead us astray. **Confirmation Bias** and **Availability Bias** are cognitive short-cuts that skew our understanding of what we are trying to research. A confirmation bias is the tendency to accept information we already believe as more relevant, and opposing arguments having less merit. Similarly, Availability Bias is the mental tick of accepting common or readily apparent information as more broadly representative of what we are studying than is appropriate. In short, if you are looking for answers, you are likely to find them. Investment research may be better served by looking for questions.

The research on behavioral finance is fascinating with many academic papers finding market-wide exploitable effects, but more relevant for this text is identifying and recognizing your own personal tendencies and being able to control or eliminate them. Emotions are not the best investment guide. Gut decisions are rarely the good ones.

What has been presented here has emphasized equities and bonds. But when we offer solutions to clients sometimes we need to have more than a generic risky and risk-free bucket. Introducing investments like hedge funds, real estate, private equity, and commodities can be sensible – only to the point it is not a distraction.

We must remember back to our financial plan there is a return bogey the client needs to achieve, and introducing new investments must not lower the expected return below that hurdle. We must also be cognizant of the risk and illiquidity that may be introduced. Market neutral hedge funds may be good at reducing volatility, but may not generate high returns. Commodities may offer inflation protection, at the cost of long periods of underperformance. Private equity may have superior returns that are only realized after ten years of locked up capital. There is always a trade off – you don't get return without some risk. By introducing different sources of return we are hoping to diversify our risks.

When we are building a multi-asset portfolio we should have an understanding of each component's role and an expectation of how it could perform over a long horizon, and in different environments. Then just as we examine the efficient frontier, we should make some judgement of whether including different investments will increase return or stabilize volatility, subject to a client's constraints. We need to evaluate whether each asset class in the portfolio is an *efficient* use of risk.

After studying the available options we can evaluate what an appropriate portfolio of multi-asset investments would look like. Does the expected return still reach the client's needs? Is the expected volatility acceptable? Unfortunately, introducing more esoteric investments clouds our ability to discern the probability of adverse results. A rock-solid hedge fund that consistently returns ~9% can suddenly lose 50% in the wrong environment.

The strategic allocations we are making are meant to serve a purpose. We are not adding complexity because it is fun, but because the portfolio we create is robust, diversified, and delivers a client's needs. Like a simple equity portfolio, it is defined with purpose. That does not mean unchangeable, we should always be aware of the changing value offered by our investment options. As we gauge the economic environment and decide which risks we want to embrace, and those best to avoid, it makes sense to adjust client allocations. But each of our investments needs a reason to be included before its purchase and not justified after.

Every wealth manager is a Chief Investment Officer of a multitude of multi-asset portfolios. As each client is different, portfolios can diverge from a standard model. What keeps the Advisor on track is knowing and understanding what is in his investment tool box. What does each tool do? When is its use appropriate?

We need to be able to look at the world around us and anticipate its dangers and opportunities, and have ready the tools that can respond. You may choose to increase allocation to an existing portfolio target, or introduce a new concept when the time is right. How active you choose to be will be determined by your approach and by the liquidity of your portfolio components.

The most difficult hazard you must navigate is not the temporary rough waters in the markets, but the unappreciated complexity you choose to bring into the portfolio: the positions you added long ago because they seemed right at the time that no longer make sense, the private equity sponsors who just extended the investment term, the hedge funds that are more market correlated than you thought. It can feel powerful to believe you have all the tools you need to manage through any environment. Having the tools does not mean you are in control of them.

WHAT COLOR IS YOUR PORTFOLIO?

This book has endeavored to present a framework to think about portfolio management with a theoretical foundation and a practical guide. The goal is to educate advisors to be able to evaluate their own investment management process. In some ways portfolio management can feel like a battle against other market participants, and these skills help define the front lines on which you choose to fight. Although we look outward for our advantage, we should be aware of our own intuitions and preconceptions that can weaken us. Behavioral finance describes how many of our trading strategies and investment approaches can be biased. But sometimes our grasp of even that which is obvious can be flawed. The following anecdotes illustrate some examples of how things that seem straightforward are actually ambiguous or counterintuitive.

In 2015 a photograph was posted on Facebook by a woman revealing the dress she would wear for a coming wedding she was attending. It was an innocuous post that created quite a stir, because some people who saw the dress determined it was a blue dress with black trim. But others were confused because they clearly saw a dress that was white with gold trim. The original image was washed out, and scientists believe that our brains naturally made assumptions and filled in the colors based on our experience. People who were more exposed to natural light during their days automatically adjusted the photo and saw a white and gold dress. People who were usually exposed to artificial light saw the true colors, blue and black. People's experience literally colored their perceptions of reality.

I heard about a man in Chicago who had two very good friends, and after work he would let chance decide whom he would visit. He would head to the train platform and decide where to go based on which train came first. Since both trains arrived at 10 minute intervals, he expected to visit each friend an equal amount of time. However he found that he visited one friend 70% of the time and the other 30% of the time. How could that be if both trains arrived at the same frequency? He realized that one train arrived three minutes after the first one, so there was a seven minute interval during which he would visit one friend, but only a three minute interval during which he would be led to visit the other.

A brain teezer was posited based on the game show Let's Make a Deal, commonly referred to as the Monty Hall Problem, named after the host of the show:

Suppose you're on a game show, and you're given the choice of three doors: Behind one door is a car; behind the others, goats. You pick a door, say No. 1, and the host, who knows what's behind the doors, opens another door, say No. 3, which has a goat. He then says to you, "Do you want to pick door No. 2?" Is it to your advantage to switch your choice?[57]

Our instincts may lead us to say that if there are only two doors left, each door has the same probability, and there is no incentive to switch, regardless of the action of the host. However, when you originally made your choice, there was a 1/3rd chance of being correct, and a 2/3rd chance of being wrong. When the host shows you a door with the goat, there is *still* a 2/3rd chance you were wrong at the time you made your choice, but that 2/3rd probability is now truncated into the one other door. Even though there are only two doors remaining, one door has a 1/3rd probability and the other has a 2/3rd probability of having a prize, and you should always switch.

These examples are interesting because the right answer not only may seem wrong, but *obviously* wrong. What does this have to do with portfolio management? We have to remember that as we make trades that diverge from our benchmark, someone else is on the other side of the trade possibly taking the opposite position. We should have the humility to evaluate our instincts.

As much as we are battling the markets to be correct, we are also battling ourselves. The managers who get it right, often have the correct **experience** to evaluate situations and can see what others can't. They are aware of **context** and know that even when probabilities indicate success, it is not all that matters. And finally successful managers can be **flexible**, and when new information presents itself, prudence dictates you change your mind.

Let me elaborate. First, experience and perspective matters. This does not mean if you don't have the experience, you are damned to make bad decisions. It just means that if someone says they are seeing a blue dress and you insist it is white, a worthwhile discussion may take place. Prior to the Great Financial Crisis, investors were pouring money into speculative mortgage assets, encouraged by AAA ratings from the rating agencies. Brokerages were very happy to sell these securities. But

---

[57] Source: Wikipedia. This statement of the problem was written by Craig Whitaker in a letter to Marilyn vos Savant's "Ask Marilyn" column in Parade magazine in Sept 1990

Jamie Dimon, CEO at JP Morgan held his teams back. Why? Earlier in his career he had seen an implosion of subprime credit and knew what could happen. His decision was not unorthodox given what he had seen before, but still an outlier. Those with experience are able to ask better questions and evaluated answers with an ear more conditioned to hearing substance. And others may not understand why those questions are asked. It is your decision whether to learn from those who have a different history, regardless of how confident you are in your own knowledge.

When we look at performance, we sometimes use historical results as our best gauge. If two trains each arrive every 10 minutes, does that not mean each is likely to arrive next? If two assets have the same historical return, are they sure to have the same performance? That answer is no. High yield bonds are an interesting case. The historical return is attractive, over 7% return on average over the last 20 years. Worth adding to a portfolio. But if the current yield was only 4% and spreads were particularly tight (very little excess yield compared to a less risky bond), are you still expected to earn a 7% return? Probably not. We must do more than know historical experience, we have to understand why and how performance occurred and compare that to the present context. Another example is the 60/40 portfolio. It is much more sensible when bonds yield 5% than 1%.

Finally, the concept of flexibility. We make decisions based on our best review of the landscape. There is no shame at all in being wrong, assuming we've made an honest effort. But the floor does shift beneath us. Do we switch? Do we decide the probabilities we originally assumed are no longer relevant. This is one of the hardest decisions as a portfolio manager. It is fraught with an admission of defeat, or a stubborn drive to be proven right. What must happen at this moment is a careful re-evaluation of our original assumptions. Did something change? Often when we are wrong it's because the facts moved away from us. We have a temptation to say it was temporary or the market overreacted. In fact, a door was presented to us and it was a goat. Will you switch?

Our perceptions and intuition may lead us successfully, but we must be aware whether it is knowledge or bias. We should review whether the opposite of our positions is also plausible, because people can look at the same circumstance and have a very different, surprising view. Mahatma Gandhi is said to have been asked "What do you think of Western civilization?" To which he supposedly replied "Sounds like it would be a great idea."

Most likely you are not the next Warren Buffett. I say that with confidence because it is statistically unlikely. As with investing, you should try to make decisions when the statistics are in your favor. Does present valuation look very different from historical norms? Does the implied growth rate seem likely? Can the current price support a disappointment? Ask questions. Know what is expected and know what could go wrong. Know what you are trying to control.

As you manage client portfolios it's your job to keep an even keel. You have a process, a worldview on the economy, a perspective on what makes a good investment that all comes together when you make decisions, pull levers, and express your views within a portfolio.

What you believe should not change based on who the client is. Your goals are to find investments that outperform with a minimum of risk. If emerging markets are good for your most risk seeking clients because they add diversification, the same reasoning makes them attractive for risk averse clients. What changes between clients is the constraints. Manage your beta, manage the clients' logistical and income needs. Work carefully to ensure your portfolios speak for you, saying what you want them to say.

Many investors think the market is in control, and they are just holding on. Rather, we control the risks we choose to take. Like the volume on a stereo we can lean into our choices, or just whisper them from a passive stance. The market may be volatile, like a daily war, but we can choose our battles.

As you embark on this effort, trying to out-think the world, remember you are competing against the world, the cumulative knowledge of every market participant. Some are indifferent investors, adding money each paycheck to their 401(k) accounts. Some are hyper-active hedge funds and high frequency traders who know a tremendous amount about their strategy, and have modeled the probability of loss and arbitrage potential on thousands of trades. With every trade, somebody is right and somebody is wrong about the direction of that asset. When you step in, you are putting your imprint on the market, your voice among millions.

Be Disciplined. A defensible process is an important guardrail. It protects you from your worst instincts and can always help explain realized performance. New funds, new vehicles, new strategies are always being presented – but as exciting as they may be your approach to portfolio management should not be compromised to make room for an untested or incompatible idea. **Be accountable**. Understand your goal is to be a good steward. If you choose to be an active investor then performance does matter, it is important, and it is your responsibility. Own what you are doing – your process and your results. **Be informed.** You will probably always know less than you'd like to know, but don't give up. Keep thinking about what you need to know more about. **Be humble.** There are many who see this as a noble calling, and many who just appreciate its promise of personal riches. **Learn from others.** Making mistakes is costly – to clients. There is so much to learn, so much we didn't even know we needed to learn, and yet much of it we can learn from others. Instead of building forts around our business and ideas, we should be open to what our colleagues have experienced, and the wisdom they can impart. **Express yourself.** If you believe something about the financial markets it should be clearly expressed in the portfolio. Your portfolio should have a narrative, it should tell a story you can explain to clients. If it sounds good to you, it will probably sound good to them because they rely on you for confidence and direction. And if the story no longer makes as much sense, it's time for the portfolio to adjust. And finally, **keep your perspective**. Market participants are trained to follow the horse race with an unhealthy and unsentimental breathlessness. Don't let your clarity be trampled by the crowd.

Many of the smartest have gone down in flames, and many of the simplest have done exceptional work for their clients. You can always marvel at how much there is to learn, you can always try harder to understand, and you can always help others along the way. And that may be the most rewarding part of being a portfolio manager.